Paul A. Doyle is author and editor of eight books, including *Basic College Skills; Alexander Pope's Iliad: An Examination by William Melmoth; Pearl S. Buck; A Concordance to the Collected Poems of James Joyce; Sean O'Faolain;* and *Evelyn Waugh.* He is currently coediting a selection of studies and commentaries about Henry David Thoreau. He is also the author of the pivotal essay on Pearl Buck contributed to the Nobel Prize winners festschrift published by Fratelli Fabbri Editori of Milan. Dr. Doyle's book about Pearl Buck in Twayne's United States Authors Series has been published in several foreign language editions.

Dr. Doyle has published articles in *The Dublin Review, South Atlantic Quarterly, Eire-Ireland, James Joyce Quarterly, Twentieth Century Literature, English Journal, The Explicator, Four Quarters, Papers of the Bibliographical Society of America,* and in over thirty-five additional journals and periodicals. He is author and coauthor of ten critical guides in the Student Outline Series including *Modern European Drama, Modern British and Irish Drama, Modern American Novel,* and *The New American Novel.* He is a reviewer for *Choice,* a Contributing Editor of *Best Sellers,* a consultant in choosing the best education books yearly listed in the *National Education Association Journal* and is the Editor of the *Evelyn Waugh Newsletter.*

Since 1948 Dr. Doyle has taught at several colleges. At present he is Professor of English at Nassau Community College, State University of New York.

*Twayne's English Authors Series*

Sylvia E. Bowman, *Editor*

INDIANA UNIVERSITY

*Liam O'Flaherty*

 108

# LIAM O'FLAHERTY

By *PAUL A. DOYLE*
*Nassau Community College, State University of New York*

Twayne Publishers, Inc.   : :   New York

823
O 33zd

gfn

TO AGATHA K. DOYLE
DUTIFUL GRANDMOTHER

# PREFACE

In surveying the field of the twentieth-century Anglo-Irish novel, Sean O'Faolain remarks, "If one were to exclude Joyce . . . and Liam O'Flaherty how little is left!" [1] While a few additional writers might be mentioned, O'Faolain's statement is indeed accurate. Yet, despite Liam O'Flaherty's importance as a contemporary Anglo-Irish novelist, his work has generally been neglected by literary critics. The aim of this study is, therefore, to remedy this neglect by surveying O'Flaherty's career as a novelist and short-story writer, by pointing out the themes and characteristics of his work, and by examining his successes and failures. The focus is, of course, placed on his most significant novels and short fiction.

Since comparatively little biographical information about O'Flaherty is available, this study also seeks to present a relatively detailed picture of the salient aspects of O'Flaherty's life so that readers may be helped in understanding his development, his subject matter, and his basic viewpoints about existence. Accurate biographical and bibliographical data about O'Flaherty have been extremely difficult to obtain. It has been no mean achievement, for instance, to learn such a seemingly ordinary biographical fact as O'Flaherty's mother's maiden name. O'Flaherty has been deliberately mysterious, vague, and contradictory about many aspects of his life and career. However, numerous letters were written to ascertain the truth and several people were personally contacted; consequently, I feel that at least 95 percent biographical certitude has been obtained. O'Flaherty himself, who has come to judge all literary critics and commentators negatively, proved incredibly uncommunicative and elusive. Nevertheless, an exhaustive study has been reached, and all possible biographical and literary data which could aid in understanding O'Flaherty's career have been incorporated. Alternate possibilities and theories are presented when incontrovertible material cannot be established. Thus, for the first time, all available material on O'Flaherty has been gathered in one place, and most of the biographical data has never before appeared in print.

I gratefully thank the Reverend William A. Gardiner of Rockwell College, County Tipperary; the Reverend John Ryan of Blackrock College, County Dublin; the Reverend J. A. Carroll, President of Holy Cross College, Clonliffe, Dublin; and Professor Thomas Murphy, Registrar of University College, Dublin, all of whom kindly supplied me with biographical and scholastic information about O'Flaherty's career. I also express gratitude to Máirin Ní Eithir, Mr. O'Flaherty's niece, who helpfully provided some rudimentary biographical data, and to Miss Elizabeth Walsh of Radio Telefís Éireann who furnished me with the data concerning O'Flaherty's story readings given on the Irish broadcasting network.

I am much indebted to Professor James Blake of Nassau Community College who translated some Gaelic materials for me and who helped immeasurably in making certain that I accurately translated some of the Gaelic matter. I also acknowledge the assistance of Professor Enrico D. Frisone, formerly of Nassau Community College, who translated the article in Italian. I most kindly thank Dr. Thomas Cahalan, Mr. Matthew F. Keating, and Miss Maureen P. Walsh. The latter gave perceptive comments about *The Informer* chapter.

My appreciation to the curator of the Colby College Library Collections, Dr. Richard Cary, should also be listed, and I cite the particular consideration given by Dr. Theodore Grieder, Head of the Division of Special Collections, and Miss E. Marie Becker of New York University Library, who helped me in using the resources of the Fales Collection. I thank too Mrs. Mary M. Hirth and the Manuscript Committee of the Humanities Research Center at the University of Texas who allowed me to examine and to quote excerpts from O'Flaherty materials held by the Academic Center Library.

I also state deep appreciation to Mrs. Elizabeth McCuen of Nassau Community College for her interest and constant encouragement and to Mr. Christopher Corbett who generously, enthusiastically, and alertly did research for this book while he was in Ireland. Appreciation is extended also to Mr. O'Flaherty's sister Delia and her husband Padriac O'Hehir who were interviewed by Christopher Corbett.

In a special category is the support provided by Agatha Kelly Doyle who, with extraordinary grandmotherly devotion, shared with me the gigantic task and indescribably heavy burden of rearing three motherless youngsters while I was doing the writing and research for this book. Truly, in the everyday herculean struggle to hold together a young family, she was for six years the only one who possessed the generosity and unselfishness to lend me a desperately needed helping hand.

## Preface

My debt to the resources of the central reference collection of the New York Public Library, the Brooklyn Public Library at Grand Army Plaza, and the Boston Public Library is considerable, and the Reid Collection of Irish History and Literature at Nassau Community College Library proved valuable and useful. Mrs. Edith Forbes, Mr. Emanuel Finkel, Mrs. Helen Iooss, and Mrs. Doris Victor, at Nassau Community College, have assisted in many ways on many different occasions, and I thank them here for their efficiency and graciousness.

P. A. Doyle

*Nassau Community College,*
*State University of New York,*
*Garden City, Long Island*

# ACKNOWLEDGMENTS

I wish to express my gratitude to the following for permission to quote from copyrighted material:

To the Macmillan Company for permission to quote from *The Martyr*, copyright 1933.

To the Devin-Adair Company for permission to quote from the preface and the narratives in *The Stories of Liam O'Flaherty*.

To Harcourt, Brace and World, Inc. for allowing me to reprint material from *Mr. Gilhooley, The Life of Tim Healy, The Assassin*, and *The Informer*.

To The New American Library of World Literature, Inc. for permission to quote from Donagh MacDonagh's essay in the Signet Classics edition of *The Informer*.

The quotations from *Thy Neighbour's Wife, The Black Soul, The Puritan, I Went to Russia, Skerrett, Shame the Devil, Joseph Conrad: An Appreciation, Two Years*, and *Famine* are reprinted by permission of A. D. Peters and Company, O'Flaherty's literary agents.

To Sean O'Faolain for allowing me to quote from his writing in *The Bell*.

To the *Saturday Review* for permission to quote from Frank J. Hynes's "The 'Troubles' in Ireland," *Saturday Review of Literature*, XXIX (May 25, 1946).

To the Viking Press, Inc. for permission to quote from Edwin Muir's *Transition*, New York, 1926.

To *The New Republic* for granting the right to print excerpts from Mary Colum's review of *Thy Neighbour's Wife*. Reprinted by permission of *The New Republic,* © 1924, Harrison-Blaine of New Jersey, Inc.

Excerpts from Liam O'Flaherty's letters to Edward Garnett are reprinted by permission of A. D. Peters and Company and the Manuscript Committee of the Academic Center Library of the University of Texas.

# CONTENTS

# CHRONOLOGY

1896    Liam (William) O'Flaherty, son of Michael and Margaret Ganly
        O'Flaherty, born on August 28, in Gort na gCapall near
        Kilmurvey on Inishmore (Aranmore), the largest of the Aran
        Islands, County Galway, Ireland.

1908–   At Rockwell College, Cashel, County Tipperary.
1913

1913–   At Blackrock College, County Dublin. While at school here, he
1914    organized a corps of Republican Volunteers.

1914    September–November, Dublin diocesan seminary (Holy Cross
        College), Clonliffe.

1914–   University College, Dublin. Joined the college corps of Irish
1915    Volunteers among whose officers was Joseph Plunkett.

1915    Left college to join the Irish Guards of the British Army.
        During the war and during part of his world traveling he used
        the name Bill Ganly.

1917    March–served in France and Belgium with the Irish Guards as a
        private in the infantry. September–wounded at Langemarck by
        a shell explosion.

1918    Invalided out of military service. Awarded bachelor's degree
        (War) from University College, Dublin, on the basis of special
        provisions for those who served in the war.

1918–   Began a period of various jobs and wide traveling in London,
1920    Brazil, the Mediterranean area, Canada, and the United States.

1921–   Involved in the Irish Civil War; supported the Republican cause
1922    against the Free State government. On January 18, 1922, he
        and several other unemployed men seized the Rotunda in
        Dublin, hoisted a red flag, and held the building for three days
        until the Free State government threatened to use violent
        measures to dislodge the insurgents. Appropriated food from
        Boland's Mills in Dublin and distributed free biscuits and bread
        in order to help alleviate starvation conditions among the poor.
        Wrote for Republican papers; participated in the Republican
        Four Courts Rebellion. Fled to England and began to write
        steadily.

1923    First published creative work—a short story, "The Sniper"—appeared on January 12, 1923, in the British Socialist weekly *The New Leader.* He used the name William for the first and last time in his writing career. From then on the Gaelic Liam became his first-name signature. *Thy Neighbour's Wife.*

1924    Returned to Ireland. Was one of the founders of the short-lived literary magazine *To-Morrow. The Black Soul. Spring Sowing.*

1924–  Several of his short stories published in Gaelic.
1925

1925    *The Informer. Civil War.*

1926    Married Margaret Barrington, the former wife of the famous history professor Edmund Curtis. *The Terrorist; Darkness: A Tragedy in Three Acts* (The play "An Dorchadas" was performed in Gaelic but published in English); *The Tent; Mr. Gilhooley; The Child of God.*

1927    *The Life of Tim Healy; The Fairy-Goose and Two Other Stories.*

1928    *The Assassin; Red Barbara and Other Stories: The Mountain Tavern; Prey; The Oar.*

1929    *The Mountain Tavern and Other Stories; A Tourist's Guide to Ireland; The House of Gold; The Return of the Brute.*

1930    *Joseph Conrad: An Appreciation.* Traveled to Russia to see Marxism at work. *Two Years.*

1931    *The Ecstasy of Angus; A Cure for Unemployment; I Went to Russia; The Puritan.*

1932    Was, along with many other prominent writers, one of the Founder Members of the Irish Academy of Letters. Separated from his wife. Their marriage had produced one child, a girl named Margaret (Pegeen). Continued to move from place to place, living mostly in England and France, but returned to Ireland periodically. *The Wild Swan and Other Stories; Skerrett.*

1933    *The Martyr.*

1934    *Shame the Devil.*

1935    *Hollywood Cemetery.*

1937    *Famine; The Short Stories of Liam O'Flaherty.*

1940–  Spent the World War II years in Connecticut, the Caribbean
1946    area, and in South America. While staying in the United States O'Flaherty preached in favor of Irish neutrality at meetings sponsored by the Irish-American Neutrality League. While in the United States he wrote several stories in Gaelic.

1946    Published some pieces in Gaelic. Read "An Beo" and several other Gaelic, as well as English, stories over Radio Eireann, beginning in 1946 and continuing from time to time until 1953. *Land.*

1948    *Two Lovely Beasts and Other Stories.*

1950    *Insurrection.*

1953    *Dúil* [Desire], a collection of most of the short stories which O'Flaherty had written in Gaelic.

1956    *The Stories of Liam O'Flaherty.* Since this date O'Flaherty has published no new work. He has been living in retirement and has spent much of his time traveling.

CHAPTER 1

# An Irish Version of the Byronic hero

## I Components of a Personality

THE FIRST significant fact about Liam O'Flaherty is that he is a
man of Aran. Born on Inishmore, the northernmost of the Aran
Islands, O'Flaherty was profoundly influenced by the bleak, rocky,
Atlantic-swept environment which is characteristic of these isles lying
off the west coast of Ireland. This area is best known to American
readers through Robert Flaherty's stirring film documentary *Man of
Aran*,[1] and through some of the writing of John Millington Synge, most
notably *Riders to the Sea* and the subjective and descriptive volume
*The Aran Islands*.

The islands are unusually wild, desolate, frequently fog-bound,
dominated by the sea and its storms. The soil is shallow and almost
treeless. Wet rocks, wind wailing, a large variety and number of birds in
continuous proximity, life reduced to bare, primitive simplicity—these
and similar aspects of Aran made Synge speak of a "universe that wars
[on the people] with winds and seas,"[2] and gave him "a strange sense
of exile and desolation."[3] In describing Nara (an obvious anagram for
the islands), O'Flaherty records that the struggle of life in such a locale
was "terribly intense. There, not only extreme poverty, but the very
position of the island foster in the human mind those devils of
suspicion and resentment which make ingratitude seem man's strongest
vice. The surrounding sea, constantly stirred into fury by storms that
cut off communication with the mainland, always maintains in the
minds of the inhabitants a restless anxiety, which has a strong bearing
on character, sharpening the wits and heightening the energy, but at the
same time producing a violent instability of temperament."[4]

"Violent instability of temperament" marks both O'Flaherty and
most of the people he writes about. Primitive and elemental passions
and qualities are allowed to dominate, and the wild winds and the

*17*

turbulent seas that often tear and pound the Aran Islands have penetrated into O'Flaherty's very marrow. He proclaims with gusto:

I was born on a storm-swept rock and hate the soft growth of sunbaked lands where there is no frost in men's bones. Swift thoughts, and the swift flight of ravenous birds, and the squeal of terror of hunted animals are to me reality. I have seen the leaping salmon fly before the salmon whale, and I have seen the sated buck horn his mate, and the wanderer leave his wife in search of fresh bosoms with the fire of joy in his eye. For me, that man is great who is his own God and the slave man is a harnessed lout who jingles the coppers of his hire in the scales of mediocrity.[5]

As a man of Aran, O'Flaherty was also influenced by the mist and fog which hangs over western Eire; and he came to be actuated by "mystical dreams and mystical terrors." [6] There is much Ossianic primitivism in O'Flaherty's makeup, a reaching back to join the bards of ancient times. The movement of nature often stirs him intensely, and ancient ruins—Aran is filled with numerous prehistoric pagan and early Christian monuments—bring forth thoughts of a mystery and grandeur which encourage dreamy imaginings and theories. Gloomy meditation becomes a favorite preoccupation.

The peasant strain in O'Flaherty is also particularly pronounced. His attitude toward the peasant varies considerably from time to time and often from page to page of the same book. He frequently expresses both admiration and hatred for the common people. They raise him to romantic exaltation, but also frequently fill him with misanthropy. In general, however, O'Flaherty is distressed by the peasants' poverty, which he personally experienced on Aran. This viewpoint becomes one of the persistent strains in O'Flaherty's thought. He is disturbed by the hard lot of the farmer and fisherman; and, although at times he glamorizes their existence, his hatred of conditions which produce "the hunger and misery in the hollow cheeks and sunken eyes of our people" [7] is a recurring emotion first stirred by his own experiences with the dismal struggle for survival on the Atlantic rocks.

While the youthful O'Flaherty was absorbing the essentially brooding and primitive aspects of life on Inishmore, a priest of the Holy Ghost order from Rockwell College in County Tipperary came to the islands in 1908 seeking likely seminarians. The young O'Flaherty had already obtained a reputation for scholastic brilliance; and, if his later reminiscences can be believed, he was also exceptional in imaginative projection. He recalls his first attempt at writing fiction when he was about seven years of age. The story concerned a peasant who murdered his wife and discovered that the most preplexing problem was the difficulty of burying her surreptitiously since she was too stout to fit into the grave he had prepared. Moreover, O'Flaherty claims that the Aran schoolmaster to whom he submitted the story gave him a thrashing for writing such an unconventional tale.[8]

O'Flaherty was pointed out to the clerical recruiter as a youngster who was particularly deserving of better educational advantages. O'Flaherty was, accordingly, taken into the Junior Seminary at Rockwell, where boys who had leanings toward the priesthood could obtain a secondary education for a small fee if tuition could not be paid. At Rockwell, O'Flaherty performed with intellectual excellence; he was especially successful in both Classics and modern languages. In a competitive examination in 1912, for example, he was second in rank in the country in his marks for modern languages,[9] and while in contests against other students, he won several money prizes for scholastic achievement.

After studying at Rockwell for five years, O'Flaherty continued his education at Blackrock College, the sister college conducted by the same order of priests.[10] Again he achieved exceptionally high grades and passed on to Holy Cross College, the Dublin diocesan seminary, in the fall of 1914.[11] The exact developments in regard to O'Flaherty's religious intentions can not be established with absolute certainty. O'Flaherty's memory is not reliable, and his later bitterness tended to becloud his precise views and movements during the period in question. He often gives different versions of particular occurrences in his life. The problem is additionally complicated by O'Flaherty's natural exuberance and by his tendency to romanticize and embellish a story. Horace Gregory, not unfairly, once remarked in this connection about O'Flaherty's penchant to tell "what seem to be magnificent lies."[12]

Nevertheless, this much is certain: in 1934 O'Flaherty wrote in retrospect that he gave up the idea of studying for the priesthood while at Rockwell. He maintained that a clerical friend persuaded him to continue his studies at Blackrock where he was a nonclerical student and not a seminarian.[13] Yet the fact of the matter is that, after leaving Blackrock, he did enter a seminary designed to prepare candidates for the priesthood. He later claimed that he did in order not to disappoint his mother who wished him to be a priest.[14] He asserts that he eventually realized that he could not continue this deception, and he then won a scholarship to University College, Dublin, where he decided to study medicine.[15]

Two factors weighed heavily with O'Flaherty during this period. First, he had become an ardent political rebel; in fact, in 1913 he organized a corps of Republican Volunteers at school. Second, he grew increasingly anticlerical, initially because he felt that the Catholic Church was too wealthy while the people were too poor. This attitude served as an opening wedge to lead him to a complete break with the church. He also came to deplore the religious authoritarianism and puritanism which were commonplace in Ireland, and he felt that many of the religious beliefs being inculcated were mere superstition.

The next sharp transition in O'Flaherty's career occurred in 1915 while he was at University College: he suddenly joined the British Army. Again the motivation involved cannot be stated with finality because O'Flaherty is contradictory on the matter, and the facts cannot be proved beyond a doubt. O'Flaherty has said in one essay that he became disillusioned with the Republican cause because its leaders appeared overcautious and reluctant to rebel.[16] In another written statement O'Flaherty claimed that he enlisted on account of a "passion for adventure."[17] Another explanation notes that O'Flaherty, who had been inattentive to his studies while at University College, had joined the army in order to save his scholarship; for students entering the army had their scholarships held over until they could resume their studies.[18] Since O'Flaherty had not been taking his college work seriously, he very possibly would have failed his 1915 examination and, hence, lost his scholarship. The most likely fact is that all three explanations—disillusionment with the Irish Republican movement, a desire for excitement, and a fear that he might not retain his scholarship—were involved in his decision to enlist.[19]

While serving with the Irish Guards in France and Belgium, O'Flaherty was shell-shocked at Langemarck in 1917; and, after considerable treatment and hospitalization, he was eventually invalided out of military service.[20] He came home from the war worn in body and mind. After recuperating in Ireland for a short time, he commenced a two-year period of odd jobs and wandering.[21] He worked as an assistant foreman in a London brewery, as a porter in a hotel, and as a clerk in an engineering firm office. Then he set sail for Rio de Janiero and became a seaman on various ships both in the Atlantic and the Mediterranean. He wandered about Canada and arrived in the United States, where he was at various times a Western Union messenger, a printer's helper, a Connecticut factory worker, and a Long Island oyster-boat crewman. During this period, O'Flaherty's brother, who had earlier emigrated to America and settled in Boston, urged him to write about his hobo life and varied experiences. At this time O'Flaherty claims he had no wish to forego his life of action and travel which he felt would be necessitated if he settled down to a writing career. His brother, however, procured a typewriter; and O'Flaherty commenced to write.[22] After completing four short stories and having them rejected by a publisher, O'Flaherty hastily ceased his literary efforts.

Weary of his continual traveling, he returned to Ireland in 1920 and soon became active in Communist activities. During the Irish Civil War he and a group of unemployed men seized control of the Rotunda in Dublin and raised the Communist flag over the building.[23] In this endeavor O'Flaherty's title was "Chairman of the Council of the Unemployed." [24] Many interpreted this act to mean that O'Flaherty hoped to start a revolution of the proletariat, but others believed that O'Flaherty merely wished to call the government's attention to the plight of the poor.[25] Free State forces surrounded the building and threatened to assault the occupants unless capitulation occurred. After holding the building for three days O'Flaherty and his followers yielded in order to avoid bloodshed. He and two associates managed to avoid the authorities by fleeing to Cork.

The O'Flaherty of this period read Pyotr Kropotkin and flirted with Kropotkin's anarchistic philosophy; but, more commonly, he veered between Socialist and Bolshevik theories. He did not, however, manage to formulate a balanced and consistent philosophy, but his principal intentions were to improve the lot of the poor and the working man. While serving with the British Army in France, he recalls that he met a Scotch Socialist and was converted to socialism.[26] Interest in the rights and welfare of the working man thus became a basic pattern in O'Flaherty's thought and was the incentive which prompted him to participate in Communist activities during the early 1920's. O'Flaherty believed that the policies of the church and of the middle-class profiteers kept the people impoverished; and, as a consequence, his sympathy for the poor was increased. Like Sean O'Casey, he maintained that the only hope for the improvement of the condition of the poor was through some form of Socialist or Communist equalitarianism.[27]

In his public pronouncements O'Flaherty continued to maintain these convictions. Writing to the *New Statesman and Nation* in 1936, he declared: "I believe that the U.S.S.R. claims the allegiance of every civilised person in the world to-day." [28] In answering an authors' poll about his attitude toward the Spanish Civil War, O'Flaherty's response was unequivocal: "I am for the legal government and the people of Republican Spain against Franco and Fascism. As an Irishman I realize that the toiling masses of Spain are waging the same struggle which we have waged for centuries in Ireland against landlordism and foreign Imperialism. . . . Long live the Republic in Spain and all over the earth." [29]

Yet O'Flaherty is inconsistent in his views about communism. In writing in a travelogue describing a visit to Russia (1931), O'Flaherty alternates between praise and condemnation of communism. Russia, he discovers, is the same as everywhere else: materialistic advancement and human selfishness are still operative and are the primary factors of man's existence. In this book he goes so far as to declare that he loathes all political systems and that the ideal of an equalitarian society is unrealistic. He asserts that he had really believed in *Liberté, Egalité,* and *Fraternité*; but, after his trip to Russia, he could never again accept this concept with quite the same fervor.

Despite this reaction, O'Flaherty was never completely able to give up the hope that equalitarianism might eventually come into general practice. O'Flaherty wanted some special Irish form of socialism. Writing in *The Irish Statesman,* O'Flaherty condemned communism in Russia as well as fascism and argued that Ireland needed a brand new system of government.[30] Since the 1920's and 1930's O'Flaherty has been heard from much less, and his recorded political pronouncements are few. In 1940, upon arriving in the United States for a visit, he did grant a newspaper interview to reporters. In this statement he predicted the end of the partition between the six counties of Nothern Ireland and Eire and declared, "If there were a labor government in England it would not maintain the partition for three hours." [31] Such a comment not only indicates O'Flaherty's continued Socialist sentiments but also demonstrates the naiveté of his political views. Anyone interested in using O'Flaherty as an exemplar of political inspiration must soon become discouraged in such an aim; for O'Flaherty is by nature too much the servant of whims and moods which continually change without logic or consistency; he is too much the scoffer and profaner to be a reliable and inspiring champion of social justice.[32]

The Rotunda-seizing episode gave O'Flaherty a nefarious reputation in Ireland; and, as he recalls, "Ever since then, I have remained, in the eyes of the vast majority of Irish men and women, a public menace to faith, morals and property, a Communist, an atheist, a scoundrel of the worst type." [33] It was at this crucial point that O'Flaherty realized that, if he recanted his highly unpopular opinions, he would be welcomed back into the fold by his countrymen and could fall into the sheltering pattern of Ireland's standard beliefs. But he refused to surrender his views to gain acceptance and security at the expense of his conscience. With Byronic loneliness, and suffering similar ostracism, O'Flaherty stood in rebellion: "Crave forgiveness? Clip the wings of my fancies, in order to win the favour of the mob? To have property and be esteemed? Better to be devoured by the darkness than to be hauled by dolts into an inferior light." [34]

In June, 1922, the fugitive O'Flaherty, garbed in a trenchcoat and carrying a revolver, arrived in Liverpool, alone, disillusioned, and without any definite means of livelihood. Yet when he made his way to London, he was encouraged to write, and a typewriter was obtained. As a consequence, he wrote several short stories and a novel, all of which were unsatisfactory. In a heavy mood of depression with his existence in London, O'Flaherty had loving thoughts of his homeland: "I thought how beautiful it would be to stand on a cliff in Aran, watching the great waves come thundering to the shore, while the pure wind swelled my lungs." [35] In the midst of this nostalgia O'Flaherty felt united with the people of his native islands and determined to write about them; he began a new novel which he claimed had two motivations: "In the first place because Synge wrote a book about one of those islands that irritated me, in as much as he failed to get the personal touch. It was written in the second place as a courageous attempt to save the Irish novel from the debauched condition of being a political pamphlet or a religious controversy, or worst of all, a literary facsimile of the third-rate music hall comedies that draw alcoholic laughter from an audience of very low intelligence. It endeavours to be a faithful picture of life as I have seen it." [36]

This novel, *Thy Neighbour's Wife,* was eventually finished, re-written, sent to a publisher, and accepted. The critic Edward Garnett, who was responsible for the publisher's acceptance of the manuscript, soon became O'Flaherty's friend and literary mentor. The dependence of O'Flaherty upon Garnett, particularly during this period, can be best observed by reading O'Flaherty's letters and postcards written to his editor. These epistles, preserved at the Academic Center Library of the University of Texas, demonstrate the fact that O'Flaherty, at this time, was writing much of his work to please his closest friend. [37] O'Flaherty immediately commenced writing his second novel, and he and Garnett worked closely in its composition. But when this book, *The Black Soul,* was received with hostility by the critics, O'Flaherty fell into a mood of extreme melancholia.

Dublin life further depressed him. He was dismayed by what he regarded as the conventionality and listlessness of the Irish literary establishment represented primarily by AE and Yeats. Sean O'Casey recalled that O'Flaherty, Brinsley MacNamara, Cecil Salkeld, and F. J. Higgins started a Radical Club to encourage new artistic ideas and support young writers. O'Casey was unsympathetic toward O'Flaherty because he believed that the latter was not only arrogant but self-seeking and that Yeats's writing was much superior to that of the rebellious novelist.[38]

Even while seeking tranquillity on Aran, he felt the hostility of the islanders, which was influenced to a considerable degree by rumors about *Thy Neighbour's Wife* and *The Black Soul*. He did not believe as the natives; he was an outcast among his own people. Again O'Flaherty could logically adopt Byronic qualities. He could again select, as he had on several previous occasions, the pilgrim of eternity choice and brood showily over his predicament.

All night I stood, trembling, beneath the tree, contemplating my destiny. Should I still hold with what remained of the spiritual fetishes of my people or cut adrift completely and stand all my life alone? . . . What horror! What loneliness! . . . An outcast hermit, who makes a god of thought and eschews all contact with the material empire of this earth, denies its gods, spits on its honours, and turns his cold, loveless eyes from mother, wife, child, friend, compatriot! Such must I become if I must win the empire of the mind which has no limits, whose beauties are unfathomable, eternal since they are not chained to time, and terrifying in their mystery. . . . To contain and nourish within me the germs of all vice as well as virtue, that I might stand beyond good and evil; and therefore be suspect to the instincts of all humble men who bow their knees and turn up their palms in beggary; held in jealous hatred by my kindred; honoured only by those most alien to my nature, since they have nought to fear by contact with it.[39]

Such passages become a commonplace in O'Flaherty's autobiographical and pseudo-autobiographical statements of these and later years. Again and again, like Byron, he parades his feelings for all to see. He becomes a sort of peasant Byron—an agonized malcontent, brooding with primal grandeur and passion. He sails "forth alone on a sea and has no port of call, no land fall, nor triumphant home-coming . . . [sailing] alone with the mutinous crew of [his] passions."[40] But he is proud of his isolation, proud of his defiance, proud of his emphasis on individuality, and proud of achieving the spirit through the flesh, crying out: "Let me be covered with contumely, so long as I can feel the stirring of my flesh and the stirring of flesh in response to my flesh. I have come back to the flesh from my journey into hell with a fiercer lust. My hands are on the summit of the wall and my eyes are blinded by the light beyond." [41]

Adding to the Byronic motif is the fact that O'Flaherty also suffers because he is the gifted intellectual and artist, a superior man who must scorn the common herd on that account alone; consequently, he is made even more isolated and lonely. But O'Flaherty also maintains that the writer can keep his self-respect only if he rebels against conformity, convention, and social respectability. The serious writer "must take care to have himself considered a rogue and a vagabond, a bawdy roysterer, an enemy of society. He must be an angel of discontent." [42] To use more recent terminology, he must be an eternal nay-sayer, a dissenter, the man who shrieks out the notes of the "Eternal No." In so doing, the creative artist gains "the cold majesty and beauty," [43] toward which his spirit eternally struggles, even though reality must never be deserted. O'Flaherty claims to have been born a mystic, but he maintains that reality must be the basis of all good writers and insists that "the only true mysticism comes through reality." [44]

Unquestionably, some of O'Flaherty's views are a pose and fit tightly with his emotion-of-the-moment romanticizing; but, in general, O'Flaherty's version of Byronic attitudes is genuine. He lived as well as publicized these attitudes in his career. Granting his tendencies to self-deception, to day-dreaming, to romanticizing, to inconsistency, O'Flaherty presented a picture of the isolated, lonely wanderer searching for both the indefinable and the unobtainable, led on by the power of his passions and instincts. As Edwin Muir remarked of D. H. Lawrence, O'Flaherty's spirit "is exalted only when it takes fire from his senses; his mind follows the fluctuations of his desires, intellectualizing them, not operating in its own right. . . . And that is because he is on the side of the instincts." [45] O'Flaherty carried over his Byronic materials and his glorification of instinct with turbulent emphasis in his first two novels, *Thy Neighbour's Wife* and *The Black Soul.*

## II *The First Two Novels*

The locale of *Thy Neighbour's Wife* (1923) is the Aran island of Inishmore, which O'Flaherty calls Inverara. The story concerns the career of a young priest, Hugh McMahon, who had given up the love of Lily McSherry in order to become a clergyman. Lily eventually marries a man whom she finds uncouth and distasteful and comes to reject her husband. Meanwhile, McMahon's passion for Lily revives; and he wonders why he did not marry her instead of studying for the priesthood. The novel follows McMahon's torment as he ponders his unhappiness. McMahon, bizarrely enough, is a Byronic hero in clerical collar.

McMahon faces a conflict between love and religion; but his thoughts, as O'Flaherty conveys them, are frequently inconsistent. If McMahon had really loved Lily with the intensity observed, it would appear unlikely that he would have ever become a clergyman; but O'Flaherty does not render this issue in a convincing manner. To the conflict between love and religion is added a third torment: patriotism. McMahon, an enthusiastic Republican, is deeply committed to the belief that Ireland should be free of foreign rule. Soon McMahon is found agreeing that the gentry, the politicians, and, to a certain degree, the clergy were holding Ireland back from freedom. Again the question arises: if McMahon felt this way, why did he deign to become a priest? It might be argued that McMahon's views changed after ordination, but the author has a narrative obligation to indicate and develop such a change logically; and he simply does not do so.

The novel pursues McMahon's inconsistencies, whims, passions, and romanticizings in detail—and carries them to the very limits of credibility. McMahon broods continuously, for he is a typical O'Flaherty protagonist—a hero in perpetual inner anguish. McMahon, for example, was

enraged because he had to confess to himself that the mere mention of Lily's name by Mrs. Cassidy had disclosed to him the fact that he had tried to hide in the morning and until now, that he was still in love with Lily. As he listened to Mrs. Cassidy talking about marriages he felt every word burning into his marrow and shouting at him: "This is not for you. You are a priest and cut off forever from marital happiness or unhappiness. Love or marriage is not for you. You are a pariah if you but think of marriage." And the thought of Mr. McSherry being the sole possessor of Lily, with full and legally defined rights to her, appeared to him now for the first time materially. He began to look upon McSherry as another one who was appointed by Divine Providence to torment him.[46]

It is stressed that McMahon is not just an ordinary man or an ordinary priest: he is an intellectual who had an exceptionally brilliant career in college. Father McMahon's plight and loneliness are increased because he is isolated not only from the peasants and the business class but from other clergymen. Everything that occurred, everything that he observed "showed him the chasm that divided him, a priest and an intellectual, from the vulgar world about him."[47] As if these difficulties were not enough, O'Flaherty has given McMahon other handicaps. For example, the priest does not drink anything of an alcoholic nature, but he can torment himself with the possibility of becoming intoxicated simply to make Lily suffer:

It would be a just punishment for Lily if her scorn for him drove him to drink and destruction. He pictured himself, coming mad with drink, laughing in her face diabolically, crying: "You drove me to this, you wicked woman, you are accursed."

As he walked towards the school he wove a romance about himself. He himself was always the central figure in the romance, the hero, the oppressed, the misunderstood, the unappreciated, the tortured.[48]

"The hero, the oppressed, the misunderstood, the unappreciated, the tortured" are proper words to describe not only the clerical protagonist but the author himself; for both protagonist and creator drive themselves into a frenzy by their moods, imaginings, and meditations. They both suffer from a sensitivity too penetrating to be borne and from neurasthenia.

O'Flaherty must do everything—no matter how improbable—to slant the situation so that McMahon's broodings can be indulged. When Lily is attracted to a dashing young rebel named Hugh O'Malley, the priest becomes fiercely jealous. When O'Malley engages in a boat race in order to demonstrate his prowess and wins, McMahon turns "black with rage. He almost hurled himself from the wall on his enemy beneath."[49] He cursed and soon took a drink (he has now turned to alcohol for solace) and exclaimed, "If I were a man I would kill him . . . and her, too."[50] Such behavior and utterances for a man of McMahon's vocation are conveyed so ineptly that he becomes completely improbable as a human being. A little later, the priest even wishes he possessed a revolver so that he could kill the two lovers.

McMahon fluctuates in his emotions throughout: one moment he is internally expressing his passion for Lily and regarding his religious calling as insignificant; the next moment he professes remorse and a feeling of guilt. In such torment McMahon emotes throughout the novel; he is a whirlwind of emotions, of conflicts, of neuroticism. But the priest eventually comes to accept the fact that he cannot now have Lily's love. His hatred of Lily for her failure to encourage his attentions and his rancor against O'Malley vanish as suddenly as they had arrived. He now can think only of entering an oarless boat in Rooruck, a remote and wild section of Inverara, and, like alleged saints of old, doing penance for his sins by sailing on the turbulent waters. Out in a frail bark he is caught in a vicious storm and runs a whole gamut of emotions from satisfaction to terror, from hope to despair. Finally, a desire to live becomes his central thought. As he cries out to God for succor, he promises in a high pitch of tension to volunteer as a missionary to China if he is preserved from death. After enduring considerable fright and the buffeting of the storm, McMahon is rescued. He is now elated, not only because his life has been spared but also because he believes that the ordeal in the storm has purified him and that his past temptations have been forever overcome and defeated. The time has now come when he can devote himself exclusively to the church. He gives up his interest in the Republican movement; he surrenders his goal to be a famous poet; he yields all claims to Lily. In the fervor of his rescue, "Nothing mattered but the Church." [51] These thoughts and feelings are the complete reverse of many of his former musings. Earlier in the book, for example, McMahon could think "everybody was anticlerical who was worth anything. What was a priest anyway? All silly rot. . . . What were dogmas? Folly and superstition." [52] In the light of McMahon's emotional gymnastics, his complete conversion to God and missionary work in China is far from convincing; and, at the end of the book, the reader stands skeptical and far removed from the protagonist.

*Thy Neighbour's Wife* fails as a novel because it does not engage the reader's sympathies. The reader stands apart from the characters and action because he is bewildered by the primitivism on display. It is as if, as L. P. Hartley was to remark about another O'Flaherty novel, the story "had been written by a cave-man for cave-men." [53] The over-all ineffectiveness of this tale of sound and fury must be attributed to O'Flaherty's tyro ineptness, and the principal form of this ineptness on display is the inadequacy of O'Flaherty's method for conveying information. He is prone to tell us baldly too much about the characters instead of letting the characters reveal themselves naturally in thought and action. The defective nature of his method is especially pronounced when he deals so fundamentally in contradictory and continually fluctuating emotions. The characters suddenly switch back and forth from mood to mood, or just as suddenly adopt a new mood or attitude.

At the beginning of the novel, for instance, the youthful Lily, who has recently returned to Inverara, undergoes a rapid change of attitude toward her husband. O'Flaherty relates this in part: "The slight, girlish form that had stood on the deck of the *Duncairn* had disappeared. In its place stood a woman, fully matured, fully developed, the lines of girlhood changed in that moment of acute distress into the mature curves of womanhood. Her black eyes were blazing. . . . Lily McSherry had ceased to be a girl. She had become a woman." [54] The point is not that such a change would not take place but that O'Flaherty fails in his hasty and impatient manner of narration to convince us, first, that it could take place and, second, that it could take place in quite the manner indicated. Further, by confining the action of the novel to eight days, O'Flaherty limits the expansiveness which the action and such a protagonist as McMahon require.

Apart from the Victorian and melodramatic flavor of the writing, the shifting and variety of emotions are not conveyed with the proper narrative artistry either to convince or to persuade. Hence, too frequently the characters appear wooden and unreal, and the action and setting are stagy and too consciously manipulated. The novel is also weighted down with too much description, and it needs much more dialogue for both variety and narrative balance. It cannot be doubted that O'Flaherty knows his setting, but doubt does arise as to whether he really knows his people. His characters are all emotion; as such, they lack dimension and credibility. To some degree, they almost seem to be will-o'-the-wisps. They have an elusiveness about them; we reach out in vain to grasp them. O'Flaherty felt that Synge had deemphasized the violent, passionate nature of the islanders, and, in general, O'Flaherty's view is correct, although Synge was cognizant of "the primitive feeling of these people . . . that a man will not do wrong unless he is under the influence of a passion which is as irresponsible as a storm on the sea." [55] Synge has perhaps made his peasants and fishermen more genteel than they really are; O'Flaherty, on the other hand, has made his islanders more violent and passionate than they really are. O'Flaherty has moved to an extreme which appears much too excessive.

In any case, O'Flaherty's first novel establishes a pattern that he usually follows in most of his future long narratives. He focuses on one central character, and this individual is presented in a vortex of emotion and turmoil. The protagonist's instincts and emotions are paramount, and they will run the whole psychological gamut being described by the omniscient narrator who seems not to be disturbed by the problem of making abrupt and sudden shifts convincing. This hero will be lonely, tormented, melancholic, a wanderer; he will have a considerable number of affinities with Byron; and, above all, he will be one and the same with Liam O'Flaherty himself.

Although less than one year elapsed between the publication of *Thy Neighbour's Wife* and *The Black Soul,* O'Flaherty's second novel is much more competent in both technique and over-all effect. Again the scene is Inverara and Rooruck, and the action occurs some undefined number of years after the events of the previous novel. There are, for instance, references to Hugh O'Malley's eloping to America with Lily McSherry; Dr. Cassidy, the physician of *Thy Neighbor's Wife,* has been forced to retire from practice because of advanced age; and Socialist John Carmody also appears in both books. Further, the character of Red John in *The Black Soul* is obviously developed—although somewhat altered—from the figure of Big John of Rooruck.

The most meaningful aspect of *The Black Soul* is its definite autobiographical parallels. The protagonist, whose name is Fergus O'Connor, but who is usually referred to throughout the book as the Stranger, is an ex-World War I soldier who retires to Aran in hopes of healing his physical and emotional illnesses. Like O'Flaherty, the Stranger remembers the horror of the dead and dying on the battlefield—three years spent in hell; he recalls "the night he was buried by a shell in France." He mentions that he wandered around the world for two years after the war "trying to find somewhere to rest," until he was instructed by his doctors to come to Inverara so that he might overcome his nervous tension and melancholia. Yet the inhabitants of the island declared "that he was mad, and had no religion." The Stranger recollects attempting "to find consolation one day in religion, the next day in anarchism, the next day in Communism, and rejecting everything as empty, false and valueless. And at last, despairing of life, flying from it as from an ogre that was torturing him, he had come to Inverara." [56] In this present mood he was disillusioned with civilization, philosophy, and culture—"only thing is to live like a beast without thought . . . not to give a damn. . . ."

Although shattered by the war and in a state of severe depression and disillusionment, the Stranger is powerful, handsome, and passionate; he is primitive and fierce, "a prey to impulses"; his relatively vague but glamorous past adds to his mystery and appeal. When he merely touches Little Mary, Red John's wife, she trembles from the passion and power in the man. He actually becomes a D. H. Lawrence gipsy or gamekeeper; instinctive, animalistic, he emits emanations of electric magnetism. Some of this emphasis is attributable to the influences of D. H. Lawrence and of critic Edward Garnett. Garnett, who advocated that writers be passionate, had served as editor for Lawrence, and was O'Flaherty's first editorial mentor.[57]

The Stranger's depression with the world continues; the universe is filled with folly; he had been just as foolish and as insane as the other inhabitants of the globe in trying to figure out the purpose of existence and the meaning of life. Life had no purpose; a man could be certain only of nature, of the earth and the sea; eventual death and oblivion dominate all.

In his melancholy and despair he thinks of suicide, but when he meets the Socialist John Carmody, who like himself was a wanderer and an outcast from society, he decides it would be more sensible to drink heavily and enjoy Carmody's companionship. In this way he could sneer at civilization and laugh at the world about him; thus he would sublimate the blackness of his soul. At every opportunity he denounces the so-called civilized world, the Irish Republican movement, nationalism, religion, anything and everything.

In the course of the novel he encounters a young schoolteacher named Kathleen O'Daly and argues these matters with her. She holds all the beliefs he rejects. In acquiring his despair and cynical nilhilism after relinquishing his youthful viewpoints (ones still held by Kathleen), he realizes that he has not improved his condition or profited in any way by his new opinions. Kathleen seems to be a spirit, rather than a woman who is bent on drawing him back to his earlier views. He fights a mighty internal battle against surrendering his present attitudes. When Kathleen attempts to interest him in religious principles, he expresses his preference to be a "primitive man." He leaves Kathleen's company in an enraged mood; and, like a primitive savage, he seduces the willing Mary. But in the whirlpool of emotion that composes his personality, he is immediately filled with remorse; for a time, guilt is his, predominant feeling. Primitive man contends with thoughtful man: the artificial, civilized, sexless Kathleen is one choice; Mary, the child of nature, is the second. Determined to win the Stranger's devotion, Mary claims she will force the Stranger to love her or she will kill him: "Her primitive soul was as merciless as nature itself. The tender growth of civilization had never taken root in her mind. Her love raged mightily. Like an ocean wave there was nothing either within her or without her to stay its progress. It must satisfy itself or shatter itself in death." [58]

The struggle between civilization and refinement, on the one hand, and nature and the primitive, on the other, continues throughout the novel. But, in addition to the contending women, the Stranger has to meet the pressures of the natural world in a Rooruck spring season. Nature is personified as a force to be reckoned with, and the Stranger's body was stirred by the sea and the wind: "Life there is only to the strong and to the ruthless. Oh, strong, beautiful sea! Hunger-inspiring! Life-giving! Oh, the icy clasp of the wind, like the stern command of a proud father."[59] And the closeness and all-embracing pervasiveness of nature on Aran is overwhelming. Nature speaks to the Stranger and advises him to enjoy life, to realize that it is good to those who reach out for the truth of the primitive and who avoid cynicism and the stifling artificiality of intellectualism. Beauty and truth, the delights of nature, the love of the elemental Mary—these are all one; and they demonstrate that nature can restore a man to health and stability.

The Stranger, however, resists the lure to immerse himself completely in the primitive, and the struggle continues back and forth as the protagonist broods and broods, tosses and turns between the enticements of both forms of life. Despair and thoughts of suicide come and go. In the hero's emotional writhings Byron's apostrophe to the ocean is recalled:

There was nothing eternal but the sea. "Ah, beautiful fierce sea," he cried aloud . . . "you are immortal. You have real life, unchanging life." And just as one morning in Canada when he had seen the reflection of a vast pine forest at dawn in the eastern sky, he had stood in awe, his imagination staggered, thinking that a new world had suddenly been born before his eyes, so now, looking at the sea, the meaning of life suddenly flickered across his mind. . . . His eyes roamed out over [the sea] . . . "Oh, to have strength like the sea," he thought. "Just to go on fearlessly until one dropped. To be ruthless. Damn conscience, honour, everything! Nothing is worth while but ruthless strength." [60]

The forces of life and nature gradually assert dominance and mastery, and love for Mary commences to win him. After Mary's husband conveniently becomes insane and dies in a frenzy, the Stranger and Mary leave Inverara for the mainland. Primitive nature, passion, and beauty are united and triumphant, and the sea can murmur victoriously: "On and on I wander endlessly. I am the lord of nature. I heal and kill heedlessly. I drive men to a frenzy and soothe others with the same roar of my anger. I am the sadness of joy. I am the ferocity of beauty." [61]

We are told that the Stranger is healed; that he fears life no more; that his doubts, broodings, and suicidal depressions are now departed. Realizing life's combination of suffering and happiness, and its conformity with physical nature, he is now ready to live. Life close to raw nature in Inverara has taught the Stranger to understand life to its marrow; and, renewed and cleansed and strengthened, he has been made whole. Nature, instincts, and passion are salvation for the individual; a Lawrentian primitivism (the religion of the blood) is extolled and recommended as the only genuine satisfaction the world can offer. Nature and the promptings of the blood triumph over the evils of civilization.

The strengths and weaknesses of *The Black Soul* are not difficult to enumerate. The book's most successful features involve the numerous richly lyrical passages describing the movements of nature, especially the water and wind. O'Flaherty is pleasingly effective when he concentrates on describing violent storms and other aspects of nature in their most primitive and turbulent forms.[62] He brings a poetic lilt and a wild musical rhythm to bear. Although at times he uses nature descriptions and lyrical prose in his first novel, such passages tended to be calculatingly set, to be overly lengthy, and to lack lilt and lyricism. In this novel the passages are richly musical and beautiful in imagery, and they seem to be more naturally a part of the context and to fit logically the over-all mosaic of the book. When George Russell (AE) declared in *The Irish Statesman* that *"The Black Soul* overwhelms one like a storm," he had in mind O'Flaherty's combination of lyrical description and the emphasis on primitive passion. AE epitomized much of the book's appeal by calling it the "most elemental thing in modern Irish literature." He maintained that the story "might be pushed back two thousand years or earlier to the time of neolithic humanity" and lauded O'Flaherty for relating the wild mood of the sky and sea so that they "echo with their wildness the passion in the heart of the characters."[63] O'Flaherty deliberately set out to capture Irish energy: he once wrote in a letter that he viewed his country's culture as "the wild tumult of the unchained storm, the tumult of the army on the march, clashing its cymbals, rioting with excess of energy."[64]

Nevertheless, the negative aspects of the book outweigh its excellence. In the first place, O'Flaherty maintains a tone throughout which is simply too high-pitched. The continuous stress on pronounced passion and emotion makes most of the characters seem one-dimensional primitive brutes.[65] Except for the character of Kathleen O'Daly, the figures in the story lack the balancing aspects of humanity which would make them appear more average, or normal, and hence more believable. This emotional-shrieking approach also gives the book a wooden, melodramatic aura. Nature is presented as extravagant and exuberant; and, given the locale, such a portrayal is valid. But the characters themselves are so exuberant that they appear out of place.

Instead of participating vicariously in the action or being involved to some degree with the characters, the reader is kept separate and aloof; and the narrative thus lacks the impact it should possess. Moreover, O'Flaherty is also too prone to use hackneyed descriptive phrases and clichés and to write stereotyped dialogue. There is a lack of freshness in style which is oddly juxtaposed among some of the most imaginative and lyrical nature descriptions in the history of the twentieth-century novel.

As was true of O'Flaherty's first novel, he has not written a persuasive ending, although the conclusion of *The Black Soul* is a bit more credible. In the first story, O'Flaherty could not project himself with complete conviction into the character of Father Hugh McMahon; as a result, McMahon's change of heart and decision to become a missionary do not persuade the reader. The Stranger's achievement of regaining his composure and the meaning of life is more acceptable because his experiences and attitudes are so much closer to those of O'Flaherty's own life. O'Flaherty eloped with Margaret Barrington, who left her husband; and the same intensity of love and passion is transposed from reality to fiction. Even granting the autobiographical similarities, however, so intense and excessive has the Stranger's rage been that, as J. B. Priestley once perceptively remarked, "it is difficult to believe that his peace of mind would last more than a fortnight." [66]

In short, then, despite O'Flaherty's lyrical gifts and despite the fact that he thoroughly knows his setting and often describes it with imaginative appeal, his characters in *The Black Soul* are just too elemental and too incredible to be taken seriously. No sense of proportion or balance exists in the primitivism and in the wild romanticism, and the excesses of which Byron and D. H. Lawrence are at times guilty are amalgamated with the neurasthenia of a sort of hyper-romantic Young Werther.

# CHAPTER 2

# The Informer

## I  *Gypo Nolan versus Gallagher*

A LTHOUGH THE events in his first two novels occurred in the Aran Islands, O'Flaherty uses Joyce's Nighttown Dublin locale as the setting for *The Informer* (1925). The episodes take place in Dublin's most squalid and disreputable section. O'Flaherty does not merely make lower-class Dublin come very much alive; he expertly blends the setting with the characterizations and the theme. This balancing of atmosphere and event is one of the most accomplished features of the book. The scene throughout is one of misery, decay, and despair; and these dominating aspects exist like a perpetual weight oppressing in some situations, while waiting to crush in other situations. All of the characters feel this wearisome burden and have been hurt by it in one way or another. The decaying buildings, the shabby flophouses, and the air of despondency and hopelessness are now ingrained in the people themselves. This place of the forgotten ones is primarily populated by degraded men and women—criminals, dope addicts, broken human souls.

In particular, O'Flaherty's Grand Guignol portraits of women re-enforce the general dreary dismalness of the setting. Such women as Katie Fox, Maggie Casey, and Louisa Cummins are viewed in the hideousness of skid-row seaminess. O'Flaherty multiplies Naturalistic detail in describing these unfortunate denizens of the slums. The women are "ravaged"; their clothing is "ragged"; their voices are horrid "croaks"; their eyes are "twitched at the edges"; and their lips are "swollen" and hanging at the sides. For Louisa, since she is the oldest, the most grotesque adjectives are reserved. Her head is "shrivelled," and her open mouth displays four widely spaced "yellow teeth," that protrude from excessively red gums. The teeth are "crooked, yellow fangs." With such detail O'Flaherty continuously keeps before the reader's eyes a wretchedness which is the natural companion of Gypo Nolan's dismal existence and eventual death.

The Civil War between the Irish Republican Army and the Free State authorities has slowed to a halt; but, although the Irregulars have been defeated, isolated rebel groups are carrying on the struggle for complete independence from Britain. Many of these organizations act independently: some are more radical than others; some are even Communist. Gypo Nolan, an ex-member of one of these Communist units, and his close friend Frankie McPhillip have been officially expelled from their cell because they were involved in carrying out an unauthorized murder. McPhillip, the actual killer, is sought by the police, and the twenty pounds' reward money looms large in Gypo's mind.

Gypo's poverty is extreme. He has no source of income, and he survives from day to day in a half-starved state. On the occasion at the beginning of the novel when he meets McPhillip, he is particularly distressed because he does not have enough money to purchase sleeping space in a flophouse. Obsessed by his immediate needs of survival, thinking only of the elemental requirements of food and lodging, Gypo informs on McPhillip in order to obtain the twenty pounds' reward. As a consequence, the police ambush and kill the fugitive; and the Revolutionary Organization, led by Gallagher, immediately hunts the informer. They eventually discover that Gypo is the culprit, pursue him, and shoot him.

By informing, Gypo Nolan commits an act considered particularly reprehensible in Ireland. As Donagh MacDonagh stresses, informing is "the unforgivable Irish sin" [1] since down through the centuries the rebel movement was constantly injured by those who thwarted its efforts by giving vital information to the authorities. Almost every revolt or carefully planned uprising had its informers, and the odiousness of such behavior so disturbed the people that even descendants of known informers are socially shunned today in parts of Ireland. "The theme of the informer in folklore, in ballads, in history, is so much part of the Irish tradition as to make the informer the unforgivable outcast." [2] Nolan has, thus, not only committed a crime against McPhillip and the Revolutionary Organization, but he has also performed an infamous act "against the steady tradition of the country."

In the descriptive and analytical portrait of Gypo Nolan, O'Flaherty has created one of his most lifelike, memorable characters. Gypo, who is about thirty years of age, is a man of huge physical proportions; but mentally he is dull-witted. Gypo's mind is cumbersome and easily muddled; he cannot think clearly for long periods; and he frequently forgets important matters, as when he forgets that he has blamed Mulligan for informing on Frankie McPhillip. Gypo cannot reflect on several ideas and weigh the pros and cons of a decision. When an idea has formed, it becomes a single-minded obsession; but he does not think matters out to their logical conclusion. He is not malicious by nature; he simply does not realize implications of his behavior or the harm that he might cause. He informs in order to obtain money for his immediate physical needs; when informing, he gives not the slightest thought to the consequences of his act of betrayal. Like the biblical Judas—O'Flaherty draws several New Testament parallels throughout the novel—Gypo does not understand the enormity of his crime or that it will result in tragedy.

When Gypo later realizes the harmful consequences of his action, he endeavors to return the money. Judas attempted to return the price of blood to the high priest, but Gypo symbolically gets rid of it in various ways. He gives four pieces of the "Judas-money," as O'Flaherty calls it, to Mrs. McPhillip in a tense and dramatic scene at her son's wake. Gypo yields the rest of the money in other ways: for alcohol, to the crowd he treats to a meal, and to pay prostitutes. Except for momentary pleasure, Gypo really obtains nothing of significance for his money. Again the analogy to Judas is underscored, for Judas also received nothing whatsoever for the thirty pieces of silver except ostracism and eventual death.

The key to Gypo's nature is that he is essentially a child, a creature of instinct and emotion. He delights in obeying impulses and operates in a "frenzy of passion." As a result, all of his decisions are spur-of-the-moment determinations, as for example, his visit to McPhillip's wake and his trip to the brothel. When he gives three pounds of his reward money to pay the fare of one of the prostitutes who wishes to return to England, he is not acquainted with her and will never see her again; yet he is capable of spontaneous generosity as well as spontaneous evil. He wears his heart on his sleeve: in Gallagher's presence, for instance, he instantly switches from anger to friendliness depending upon Gallagher's attitude. His behavior reminds the reader of children who suddenly quarrel with their intimate playmates and soon forget their differences and return to the previous state of friendship; but it is too late for him to revert to a state of friendship with McPhillip. And when Gypo also impulsively treats a crowd of people, most of them strangers, to a meal, he feels important; he reaches a sort of king-of-the-children level of thought.

Another indication of Gypo's childlike qualities is his compulsion to wear his hat or have it readily available. The hat becomes a security rag or teddy-bear symbol of childhood needs (at one point he becomes frantic when he temporarily loses the hat) and of his limited mental and emotional development. Nolan's pleasure in violence and fighting—in showing his muscle—is also an example of the childlike attitude of showing off, of demonstrating physical strength. As is true of the majority of male protagonists in O'Flaherty's novels, Gypo is, like so many grownups, essentially a child. He is as savage and irrational, as subjective and as impulsive, and as impractical and as romantic as a youngster.

Although Gypo Nolan has committed a heinous deed, he retains sympathy because of O'Flaherty's handling. Gypo is portrayed as worthy of compassion since he is observed in all his undeveloped mentality, childlike simplicity, and human weakness. Even his enemies in the Revolutionary Organization, who must exterminate him, can observe his real nature:

The sight was fearsome even to the callous men that surrounded him. Even *their* hardened souls saw a vision of a strange life just then, an unknown and unexpected phantom that comes to some once in their lives and that never comes to many, the phantom of the human soul stripped naked of the covering of civilization, lying naked and horror-stricken, without help, without hope of mercy. They forgot for the moment their hatred of him. They forgot that this helpless, shapeless mass of humanity was a menace to their lives. . . . They only knew at that moment, that he was a poor, weak human being like themselves, a human soul, weak and helpless in suffering, shivering in the toils of the eternal struggle of the human soul with pain.[3]

Nolan is presented as a symbol of suffering humanity, and forgiveness becomes the central issue of the novel. Gypo eventually seeks to obtain forgiveness since he is genuinely sorry for what he has done, and Mrs. McPhillip (who symbolizes Christ's mother, Mary) forgives Gypo's act of betrayal. Sorrow and forgiveness thus conjoin in the denouement. Mary McPhillip is most admirable when she behaves with understanding toward Nolan. Her intuition tells her that Gypo is guilty of betraying her brother, but she is too tenderhearted, too forgiving, and too generous to act against him. In this behavior she represents a more balanced humanitarian attitude which contrasts sharply with the lack of sympathy characteristic of Gallagher, the one man to whom she wishes to give her love.

When Gypo collapses and dies, his limbs are stretched out in the form of a cross. The Christ allusion is intended to re-enforce the notion that all humanity suffers intensely; that, as such, everyone is a Christ; and that compassion and forgiveness are vital necessities of existence. Gypo—like all humanity—has within him both Judas and Christ. He betrays; he suffers; he can be saved through forgiveness. Mrs. McPhillip's statement "I forgive ye. Ye didn't know what ye were doin' " is a conscious echo of Christ's "Forgive them, Father, for they know not what they do." Although Frankie McPhillip's mother is a devoted Catholic and the last scene of the novel takes place in a church, the conclusion is in no way sectarian. O'Flaherty is not espousing Roman Catholicism or preaching a strictly spiritual theme. He is declaring that human beings are weak and pitiable, that they should seek forgiveness for evil deeds, and that forgiveness so sought should always be extended to the seeker. This is the "message" of the book, although message is too strong a word since such ideas remain implicit. O'Flaherty is, however, obviously using simple New Testament allegory to raise *The Informer* from a suspense "chiller" to the level of a parable with universal applications.

The character of Gypo Nolan is antithetical to that of an equally fascinating figure, Dan Gallagher, the commandant of the Revolutionary Organization to which Gypo formerly belonged. Gallagher is presented as cruel, ruthless and without even a modicum of compassion. Gallagher does not have the ordinary justifications for his behavior since he is not motivated by rebel patriotism and the necessity for freeing Eire from British rule. A figure such as Donovan in Frank O'Connor's "Guests of the Nation" can be cold-blooded about killing because he is dedicated to driving out the oppressors of his country; Gallagher has no such excuse.

Although he calls himself a "revolutionary Communist," [4] Gallagher is not motivated by a struggle for working man's rights. Primarily—like Luzhin in Dostoevski's *Crime and Punishment*—he is driven by selfish personal motives; he wants power for himself, although he is unable to explain his behavior satisfactorily: "I have no mercy. I have no pity. I have no beliefs. I am not master of myself. I am an automaton. I am a revolutionary. And there is no reward for me but the satisfaction of one lust, the lust for the achievement of my mission, for power maybe, but I haven't worked out that yet." [5]

On the biblical plane, Gallagher serves—primarily in relation to Gypo—as a Caiphas-Pontius Pilate symbol to the Christ-Judas elements within Nolan. Gallagher is a diabolically cruel Caiphas who treats Gypo with contempt and mocks him, and he is Pontius Pilate in pronouncing the sentence. He is both judge and executioner.

Gallagher possesses considerable animal magnetism. A stern and assertive figure, he easily attracts followers. Although intelligent, he is not a thinker in a systematic philosophic sense. He is almost a dehumanized robot, with a concentration-camp mentality; he believes in nothing and is incapable of pity of any sort. He alone enjoys Gypo's agony since hatred predominates in his makeup, and he cannot offer love to Mary McPhillip, to whom he is nevertheless attracted, because he does not believe in love. Yet, as is true also of Gypo, he is a creature of emotion and possesses the frenzy of passion so typical of most of O'Flaherty's fictional figures.

Gallagher's attitude may be most accurately described as nihilistic, but his nihilism has been arrived at more through instinct and environmental influence than through intellectual meditation and development. In origin, Gallagher, the son of a Kilkenny peasant who had destined him for the priesthood, was expelled from a seminary after striking one of the clergy during an argument. As a result, Gallagher has had relatively little formal education; and he has drifted aimlessly until he found a niche in this particular unit of the rebel group. Despite his qualities of leadership and his outward show of self-confidence, Gallagher is weak and unsure of his philosophy. He knows in general that he wants personal power and that he is against the idea of property; but, beyond these notions, his concepts are relatively inchoate. Of various theories he comments more than once, "I haven't worked that out fully yet." He repeatedly speaks of his feelings and his impulses which are driving him to a mysterious "new consciousness." But, if he meditated deeply and pondered these matters at length, he would have no time for action; and he regards action as too vital and important to be put aside.

While the "impulses" and "feelings" which direct and dominate Gallagher are vague and unexplained, he is very clearly conceived and presented. Although he is a Caiphas without pity and in his almost robot-like behavior he appears inhuman, he is placed before us in such an objective and vital manner that he does not forfeit complete and total sympathy. He is trapped in the same cruel society that has scarred Gypo. Lack of education and lack of opportunity to think out and express his thoughts clearly have turned him to physical violence as an outlet for expression. He has directed his frustrations into a channel which gratifies his own needs and gives his uncertain self-image an avenue of expression.

Gallagher, therefore, for all his hard-heartedness and cruelty does not emerge as a thoroughgoing villain, even though, as will be observed,

O'Flaherty's original conception of him was much blacker. Gallagher is seen as a revolutionary leader who has a job to do and does it. Gallagher must make certain that Gypo is killed because the latter has committed a crime against the revolutionary cause; for, unless the informer receives punishment, the whole rebel movement could break apart. The author accords Gypo sympathy, but his death becomes a necessity. Gallagher is observed in all his cold-bloodedness; but, since he is a credible character in a credible situation, the author's understanding is obviously extended to him. O'Flaherty knows the Gallagher type, understands him—as much as such an individual can be understood—and describes him with all his inconsistencies and complexities.

As the story develops, the real villain is life itself, or rather what men have made of life. The villain is poverty; it is also slums, hunger, all the deprivations—mainly social and economic—from which man suffers. This is the web in which Gypo and Gallagher are trapped and from which Mary McPhillip hopes to flee: "the hated association of her slum life with its squalor, its revolutionary crises, its damnable insecurity, its soul-devouring monotony." [6] The slums become the biblical Haceldama, the Field of Blood. Although O'Flaherty does not preach or moralize, it is apparent that he regards his characters as victims of economic forces and believes that only the individual expressions of this victimization vary. All are trapped in an unjust situation over which they have little control and which seeks to destroy their basic humanity at every turn.

Such a society must breed eye-for-an-eye, tooth-for-a-tooth situations. One murder leads to another; there is a chain reaction of violence, cruelty, evil, and injustice; and *The Informer* reflects a basic disillusionment with such an existence. While pity and forgiveness are seen to be highly desirable virtues, it is difficult for such qualities to flower and be maintained in an atmosphere steeped in misery and squalor.

Although the novel focuses its main attention on Nolan and Gallagher, the other characters are also observed with considerable insight and sympathy. Drunkards, prostitutes, dope addicts, and down-and-outs are described in vignette form. Katie Fox, Gypo's nominal girl friend, notifies the Irish Republican Army group of his whereabouts and is, consequently, responsible for his death. On quick reading, her act might seem slightly motivated and even improbable; but her conduct is actually most human and understandable. First, she has become very much distressed by Gypo's neglect of her when he possesses the reward money. (Although he spends it very freely, she actually derives only a trifle from his financial improvement.) Second, she is horrified by the magnitude of his sin of informing, thereby aiding Ireland's enemies; and, third, she is heavily under the influence of drugs when she gives Gallagher's rebel group the vital information they seek.

Equally as vivid and as striking as the portrait of Katie Fox is the sketch of Connemara Maggie. Maggie, a prostitute, has not fallen to Katie's level of degradation because of her more easygoing temperament and her more robust rural characteristics. Large-boned but handsome, obese but appealing, Connemara Maggie is presented as a healthy peasant, soft and rough, gentle and quick-tempered. Although she appears in the novel for only a brief time, she brings a note of stability that is soon to fall into corruption because of the present environment: "She seemed to be, like Gypo himself, a child of the earth, unconscious of the artificial sins that are the handiwork of the city." [7]

The various members of this particular revolutionary organization unit are also skillfully portrayed. With one exception, these rebels are not unselfish, high-minded men. Mulholland, for example, wants prestige and advancement. (He seeks promotion to McPhillip's vacant council spot.) Peter Hackett is a member because he worships Gallagher as a hero and because it is fashionable to be a rebel and be one of the group. (Gypo's motives for becoming a member of the rebel organization are never explained, but his reasons were unquestionably similar to Hackett's.) Lawrence Curley is a member because he is a dissident and a crank; and, although he is disliked by everyone for his extremist views, he has to find a home and identify with something concrete.

The only organization member who approaches some degree of idealism is Dart Flynn, who both believes and preaches his Communist faith, although he has "no moral sense." Of the cause and for the cause in theory and practice, he lives an ascetic existence, and he gives most of his earnings to hungry street urchins. Although he is delineated in a succinct sketch, Dart Flynn burns into the mind; and this result is again a tribute to O'Flaherty's vivid description displayed throughout the book. Vivian Mercier's observation that O'Flaherty writes rather for the eye than the ear and that his talent is strikingly cinematic is especially apropos of this novel.[8]

## II   O'Flaherty versus the Novel

In view of the compelling reality of such characters as Flynn, Curley, Gallagher, Nolan, and the others, and in the light of the convincing portrait of the squalid Dublin "Monto" district, it is painful to record O'Flaherty's later comment about his third novel. O'Flaherty had come to believe that the most substantial and finest of his first three novels was *The Black Soul,* and he was infuriated with the critics who were adverse to this particular book.[9] He claimed that the critics had in effect killed him, and he fiercely denounced them declaring that they did not possess "sufficient blood ... to contract syphilis."[10] O'Flaherty, therefore, was doubly enraged when the critics joined in almost unanimous and enthusiastic praise of *The Informer,* a work he considered inferior to his pet novel of passion on the Aran Islands.

O'Flaherty took the critics to task for praising the reality and verisimilitude of setting and characters since he later claimed in a pseudo-autobiographical work to have taken the "facts" of *The Informer* from "happenings in a Saxon town, during the sporadic Communist insurrection of about nineteen twenty-two or three."[11] Since the accuracy of the Dublin setting can be verified and since such types as Gallagher, Flynn, and Curley (Curley's spiel consisted of such words as "The red flag will be hoisted any minute") existed in O'Flaherty's period in Dublin (and O'Flaherty and his followers, it will be remembered, actually raised the red flag over the Rotunda), it is evident that O'Flaherty is deliberately attempting to mislead the critics and make them look foolish. His additional comment that he deliberately set out to trick the critics must also be regarded with considerable skepticism since a statement that the material in *The Informer* had "hardly any connection with real life" is too obviously contrary to the facts to be accepted.[12]

Nine years after *The Informer* was published, O'Flaherty asserted that he wrote this novel as a sort of confidence trick in order to make money and fool the critics whom he realized would applaud the book.[13] Yet such statements are contradicted by O'Flaherty's letters to Edward Garnett written at the period when *The Informer* was projected and composed. Throughout the Garnett correspondence we hear nothing about tricking the reader or bamboozling the literary critics but only statements of seriously motivated intentions and standards.

O'Flaherty's original title for *The Informer* was *The Vendetta* and he intended it to be a "thriller."[14] He was restless to commence writing since the character of Gypo constantly obsessed him and haunted his mind, parading "with ponderous movement, scowling, shaking his tremendous head, yelling now and again. I really will weep when I kill this beautiful monstrosity."[15]

On September 18, 1924, he writes to Garnett that he is working diligently on the novel and he relates his plan and intentions:

I have envisaged a brutal, immesnely [*sic*] strong, stupid character, a man built by nature to be a tool for evil-minded intelligence. The style is brutal at that stage, without finesse, without deviation, without any sweetness, short and curt like a police report. Then as other characters appear on the scene the character of the man changes gradually. Elements of cunning, of fear, of struggle that is born of thought, appear in him. The style changes to suit this, almost imperceptibly. More and more characters appear. The character is no longer brutal. Sympathy veers around and stands in the balance for him or against him. He is now a soul in torment struggling with evil influences. At this point the style becomes definitely sypathetic [*sic*], lengthens itself out, softens, strikes a note of joy in the eternity of nature. Scenes of horror and sin present themselves.

Then with gathering speed The Informer is enmeshed by his enemies. His vast strength crumbles up overwhelmed by the gathering waves of inconquerable intelligence. He stands alone, without the guidance of a mind to succor him, seeking no outlet for his useless strength, finding that it is no longer strength but a helpless thing, a target for the beings that press around to harass it. Intelligence, evil intelligence is dominant and supreme, civilisation conquers the first beginnings of man upwards.

Then the Informer makes a last effort to escape. Here the style completely changes and becomes like a wild storms [*sic*], cascading, abandoned, poetic. From there it rises rapidly to a climax at this point. . . . After that I strike a note of pity and finish on it.

While O'Flaherty's plan of composition did not succeed in some particulars—for instance, Gallagher does not seem quite as symbolic of evil-minded intelligence as he was originally intended—it becomes evident that O'Flaherty's intention in writing the book was dominated by only the highest and most dedicated artistic intentions.

In addition to winning the applause of the critics, *The Informer* won the James Tait Black prize in England for the best novel of the year. It also won a prize in France and was widely circulated on the Continent. When in 1935 John Ford's production won the Motion Picture Academy award as the best movie of the year, the continued publicity assured the story of further reputation.[16] Yet, as is the case with many authors, O'Flaherty resented that success and popularity should come to a book he regarded as inferior to some of his other works. To be regarded as a one-book writer added distress since the continued prestige of this novel over-shadowed even a later epic work like *Famine* (1937).

Despite O'Flaherty's opinion, *The Informer* remains one of O'Flaherty's most significant books not only because of the accuracy of characterization but also because of the writer's ability to render fully and convincingly a particular time and place. *The Informer* also evinces three additional qualities at which O'Flaherty excels: first, the ability to tell an effective story in the "thriller tradition" with much suspense; second, the ability to present a scene with unusually vivid concreteness demonstrating a debt to Dostoevski and Zola in whose Realistic and Naturalistic tradition of narration O'Flaherty is working; third, the talent of probing the psychological states of his central character. O'Flaherty at his best fathoms with conviction the various emotional states and vacillations of his protagonist and extracts the struggles of the mind and spirit. As one critic observes, *The Informer* is related "with a profound command of the Judas psychology." [17]

In this psychoanalytic approach to his material, O'Flaherty is obviously working under the influence of Dostoevski, with whose work he was most familiar. Both writers are attempting much the same thing, but Dostoevski is superior in artistic handling and in emotional impact because he explores and delves deeper into characterization and demonstrates more time and patience while analyzing and examining the various ramifications of thought and action. O'Flaherty endeavors to relate his narrative quickly; he wants to push the story to its finish; and, he does not, therefore, involve the reader as internally and as thoroughly with the central characters as does his Russian counterpart. As a consequence, the reader does not achieve the same level of understanding of Nolan as of, say, Raskolnikov.

But in both instances considerable sympathy and empathy are aroused, and the psychological realism rings true. Both authors are also adept at bringing about pity although, at the commencement of *The Informer* and *Crime and Punishment*, neither protagonist appears to merit much sympathy. In addition to examining more deeply and more carefully the recesses of the mind, Dostoevski usually deals with more cerebral characters and this enables him to develop the psychological approach more effectively. Finally, Dostoevski's most obvious superiority to O'Flaherty rests in his over-all philosophy of life. Dostoevski extols love while in general, and in his characters—*The Informer* is an exception in this regard—O'Flaherty stresses violence and hatred; his work is filled with *saeva indignatio*. Perhaps the essential reason *The Informer* is such a superior work in the O'Flaherty canon is that pity and forgiveness are allowed to play a prominent role; and, even in the midst of the harshest kind of cruelty and reality, the higher qualities and aspects of humanity find expression.

### CHAPTER 3

# The Early Short Stories

## I  Man and the Forces of Nature

WHILE O'FLAHERTY produced novels in his early literary career, he also published a considerable number of short stories. His most significant work in this genre was gathered into three highly successful collections: *Spring Sowing* (1924), *The Tent* (1926), and *The Mountain Tavern and Other Stories* (1929).

"Spring Sowing," the title story of the first compilation, is a simple parable of man's existence—a composite of human duties, sorrows, satisfactions, and ultimate death. Martin and Mary Delaney, who are participating in their first seed planting since their recent marriage, perform the time-honored ritual with notable enthusiasm and even holiness. The difficulty of the work blends with the requirement for such efforts. All of the valley farmers are taking part in the yearly sowing, but the Delaneys derive more enjoyment from it because they are laboring together under the bloom of their love. Yet they must perform this task until they are aged; and, as time passes, the thrill and novelty of new love will disappear and the task of planting will not be so pleasurable as it presently is. When the couple become elderly, the ritual will be passed on, and the Delaneys will thus become like the old grandfather in the story, who, no longer able to work and bent double with age and the ravages of intense physical toil, now scrutinizes their efforts and offers advice which is not taken. He can only meditate on the eternal feeling that in the olden days the work was performed more efficiently.

Despite the laborious toil and monotony of yearly planting and farmwork in general, such labor is a necessary obligation of earthly existence. Joys and suffering, the uncommon and the mundane, combine. The young farm couple understand the value and concomitant effort of planting; they realize that they are in communion with nature in performing an act not only vital, but, to some degree, mystic and holy. By sowing, both they and nature are fulfilling primeval obligations—a covenant which is an intrinsic part of living. Their marital union is also hallowed and perfected by their joining in the traditional task before them, and accomplishment with the soil gives a unique form of satisfaction.

Mary is aware, however, that, even though she and her husband are now in harmony with the earth, the earth is hard and cruel, and is, in reality, their master. She foresees that they will be bound to the earth forever and that even in death the earth will achieve the ultimate triumph. But, in the ecstasy of young love and in the freshness of the soil, the thought of death becomes subordinated. The spring season, too, with its sense of freshness, birth, and renewal focuses reflection on the present meaningfulness of sowing and not on the future of oblivion.

This story, although set in the Aran Islands, possesses a universality for all rural times and places. It speaks of the perpetual ritual of planting and reaping, youth and age, birth and death which bind man to the earth. It is representative of O'Flaherty, in Vivian Mercier's phrasing, "as the celebrant of timeless mysteries—mysteries rooted in Nature and in that portion of Nature embodied in the life of Man." [1]

"Going Into Exile" is another parablelike tale that touches on everlasting matters. A celebration of dancing, singing, and enjoyable conversation takes place at the Feeney cabin. But, although the scene appears gay and carefree, it is underscored with sorrow because Patrick Feeney's oldest children, Mary and Michael, are to travel to the United States the next day in order to seek employment. The happiness is forced and false, the singing, dancing, and laughing are attempts to mask the melancholy. From time to time, the father leaves the seemingly joyous house in order to visit the pigsty where allegedly one of the animals is ill. In reality, he is pondering diverse thoughts which wander about in his mind. He wonders why Michael has to leave his native area when he works so industriously with the soil and is perfectly adapted to life on Inverara. The father reflects that he might never see his son and daughter again. These and similar meditations trouble him, but he is not able to articulate the many thoughts which race through his mind.

Both father and son are conscious of the difficulty of restraining their expressions of sorrow and loss at the leave-taking, yet the facade of casualness is displayed so that the departure will appear somewhat less disturbing and final: "Each hungered to embrace the other, to cry, to beat the air, to scream with excess of sorrow. But they stood silent and sombre, like nature about them, hugging their woe." [2] This same situation pertains to the whole family: sadness, hope, ambivalence are intermingled. Although the twenty-one-year-old Michael and the nineteen-year-old Mary are distressed because they have to leave their parents and friends on the Aran Islands, they feel the thrill of going to a new country; the lure of adventure stirs in their hearts. Necessity and youth struggle with homey affection and tenderness, yet nothing can be resolved. The tragic inexorability of departure and of exile—perhaps forever—cannot be assuaged. O'Flaherty controls the narrative masterfully, for the "eternal note of sadness" is present but never illogically presented or improbably exaggerated. Frank O'Connor observes that O'Flaherty treats "the nature of exile itself: a state of things like love and death that all men must in some way endure." [3] Only time and patience and endurance, as the aged peasant woman in the story declares, can ease the present unhappiness and sense of emptiness.

The narrative "Red Barbara," which considers man in conjunction with natural aspects of life that human beings cannot fully understand, is a folk fable with allegorical meanings. When Barbara Feeney, a young widow with splendid Titian hair, marries a weaver, she must adjust to the fact that her new husband is a more genteel and civilized individual than her first mate. Joseph, her second husband, remodels the run-down home of his wife, making the ramshackle dwelling a sight of beauty. He builds flower gardens and well-planned walks, so that the house becomes a village landmark. In addition to his aesthetic endeavors, he is a serious and industrious worker, and his business thrives.

Whereas Barbara's former husband had been shiftless and alcoholic, Joseph is a quiet, studious man who likes to read and who enjoys tranquility and stability. But Barbara gradually comes to be repelled by her husband; she, presented as a typical islander, primitive and earthy, finds that Joseph is too tame and well-mannered for her taste. Although Barbara's previous husband, a fisherman, had often been violent and had beaten her when he was intoxicated, she enjoyed such treatment and met him with passion on his own level. Barbara, who had had several children by her first husband, is unable to conceive with Joseph. She arrives at the conclusion that her present husband "was like a priest, an educated man who read books and spoke to the people with authority." [4]

The neighbors begin to gossip, for in this part of Ireland a husband and a wife without children are regarded with suspicion and aversion. Moreover, child-bearing is considered a duty and a necessity. As a result of the neighbors' attitude and his inability to produce children, Joseph soon begins to grow depressed and angry. As time passes, disappointment and dissatisfaction rankle, and the husband becomes unstable and eventually dies in a frenzy of despair. When Barbara marries a third time, she has children by this husband; and again she is happy and carefree although she often has to lead her newest spouse "staggering from the town, singing drunkenly, to her wild bed." [5]

O'Flaherty is once more probing the affinity between man and nature. He stresses, as did Emily Brontë in *Wuthering Heights*, that the wild and the primitive individuals, such as Red Barbara, are best matched with their kind, that nature in its most elemental state should not be thwarted by the artificialities of civilization. Earthiness exists as a fundamental and necessary aspect of the life of man. If human beings move too far away from animal instincts and requirements, they become tamed by a falsity which scars and blights their life. To be perfectly happy, man must retain his close-to-nature characteristics, remaining attuned to the heartbeat of Mother Earth.

Joseph, Barbara's second husband, is too refined and civilized, too artificial, too far from the necessary fundamental forces of nature to be acceptable to raw nature itself. Joseph, who has overemphasized things of the mind, has not maintained the necessary balance between mind and body; consequently, he is not in tune with nature and must perish. This story bears an obvious "language of the blood" influence of D. H. Lawrence, and O'Flaherty is pointedly propagating a trust-the-blood-but-distrust-the-mind point of view. Overintellectualization results in sterility and distortion—in tragedy of one sort or another. The instincts must not be unduly thwarted or treated in such a manner as to deaden their impact.

But the D. H. Lawrence influence is re-enforced by O'Flaherty's background as an Aran Islander. Even Synge once observed that on Aran "one is forced to believe in a sympathy between man and nature." [6] Red Barbara is honored in O'Flaherty's handling because she maintains this closeness. This same juxtaposition of nature and the artificial is proclaimed in "The Tramp." The title character, dirty and unkempt, appears at a workhouse hospital and encounters Michael Deignan and John Finnerty. Both Deignan and Finnerty are educated men who keep themselves aloof from the other paupers; but, when the tramp offers them cigarettes, they converse. The tramp is merely spending the night at this hostel; he plans to leave the next day and continue his traveling through the countryside.

Deignan, who has spent many months staying at the workhouse, has failed at everything he has tried since he left college. Before seeking refuge at the workhouse, he had lived idly and shiftlessly while deriving his support from his mother. Both he and Finnerty have nothing seriously wrong with them and are free to leave at any time, but are sensitive thinkers who are depressed by the problems of the world. Finnerty wishes he could have been nothing more than a simple farm laborer without worries. He has spent much money on women and drink and has used up a legacy of five thousand pounds from his aunt.

At the paupers' hospital, Deignan and Finnerty are distressed by the small amount of food available. They are usually unable to satisfy their appetites and mention this difficulty to the tramp. He informs them that he is never hungry, that he can always obtain enough to eat. He has brought food to the workhouse; and, when he leaves the hostel and gets out into the green open countryside, he intends to sit by the wayside and cook a tasty dinner. The sun, rising in the sky, promises a spring day. The tramp endeavors to interest his two new acquaintances in his joyous manner of existence: "Wouldn't ye," he inquires, "like to be walking along a mountain road with a river flowing under yer feet in a valley and the sun tearing at yer spine?" [7] The tramp feels that, like himself, Deignan could enjoy the lure of the road and insists that neither he nor Deignan are intended to be respectable citizens. Deignan, however, is too timid and too concerned about artificial matters to allow himself the freedom for a life with nature.

The tramp, who has been wandering for twenty-two years, is close to the beauty and freedom of nature, to the rivers, and to the fields: "I'm proud to say that I never did a day's work since and never did a fellowman an injury. That's my religion and it's a good one. Live like the birds, free. That's the only way for a free man to live." [8] The tramp's approach to life is appealing to Deignan, but he cannot give up his notions of civility and respectability. (Living in a paupers' hostel he regards ås a higher activity than that of being a tramp.) When the tramp leaves to continue on his way, the two educated men, who have not been able to live their lives successfully, are left bleak and hidebound while the tramp, who lives in tune with nature, is exalted and content. Conformity and so-called respectability are seen to lead to unhappiness; at least in this situation the natural man is the satisfied man. Society being what it is, the natural men are going to be relatively few; and, when they move among the "towny people" (a term used by the tramp), they will be outcasts and misunderstood.

In "The Landing," which depicts conflict with nature and its malevolence, a sudden storm arises and catches a fisherman's curragh in turbulent waters. While the villagers gather near the shore and watch the boat's struggle against the waves and wind, a threefold sweep of force envelops the scene: the power of the storm itself, the courage and skill of the fishermen struggling to reach the shore safely, and the empathic emotion welling from the watchers secure on land. As the boating men succeed in besting the turmoil, all three groups "mingled together for a wild moment in a common contempt of danger. For a moment their cries surmounted the sound of the wind and sea. It was the defiance of humanity hurled in the face of merciless nature." [9]

As this story suggests, O'Flaherty recognizes that nature is ambivalent. One of the peasants on shore, aged Bridget Conlon, remarks, "sure, we only live by the grace of God ... with the sea always watching to devour us. And yet only for it we would starve. Sure, many a thing is a queer thing, sure enough." [10] Nature both takes and gives in O'Flaherty's stories; and, although humans should strive to live in harmony with it, mankind must on occasion fight and resist it in order to survive a little longer.

This particular narrative contains one of the most effective descriptions of a sea storm ever recorded in a short story. In passages worthy of Joseph Conrad, the reader not only sees but feels and tastes the fury of the wind and water and he understands and admires the endurance of men pitted against seemingly impossible odds. Even when O'Flaherty is writing terse, realistic, primarily descriptive short stories, *admiration* for the primitive and *respect* for those who live close to nature and its elemental instincts and passion becomes the thematic motif.

For instance in "The Tent," a tinker and his two wives, who are spending a night by the side of a mountain road, take refuge in their tent during a rainstorm. During this time Carney, an ex-soldier, who is wandering about the countryside looking for work, is tramping the roads after having been fired from a job in Dublin because he did not belong to a union. Although he regards himself as vastly superior to tinkers, no other shelter is apparent so he asks to be admitted and is taken into the tent. He shares a bottle of whiskey with the three occupants, and they give him supper. After the meal and the drinking, Carney attempts to embrace and kiss one of the tinker's companions; but Byrne, the tinker, gives him a severe thrashing by fighting and wrestling in the most unsportsmanlike manner possible. The women laugh hysterically as Carney is trounced. After the traveler is prone on the ground and motionless, the tinker picks him up and throws his body away from the campsite. When Carney finally manages to get to his feet and stagger on his way, he hears the woman he had kissed scream as the tinker exacts vengeance on her because of her disloyalty.

Although the tinkers are a wild and savage lot, they, in harmony with their environment, represent the natural, elemental forces of life. Carney cannot understand them because he has not been living long enough in conjunction with nature. The tinkers, however, represent another Lawrentian glorification of the primitive, savage forces which underlie all living. For O'Flaherty, the tinkers take on a naturalness which is understandable and particularly refreshing in contrast to the false artificiality and conventions which often dominate men's lives.

In the title story of *The Mountain Tavern* collection, O'Flaherty turns to the tragic Irish Civil War for subject matter. In the years of relative tranquillity the tavern, which represented a refuge of comfort and security, had yielded a fundamental natural joy and solace. Now the tavern, wrecked and made desolate by the ravages of warfare, can give no respite to wounded and battle-worn soldiers; and its owners are bitter and disillusioned at the destruction that has been wrought. The building symbolizes Ireland during the war between the Republicans and the Free State forces. The scene is one of emptiness, ruin, and desolation, a place where now there is only death and alienation; and confusion characterizes every phase of existence. Nature itself adds to the story's motif since the snow which pervades the story also becomes a symbol for the despair and death which now dominates and victimizes Eire.

O'Flaherty's other standard stories are vignettes of country scenes and country people. Many of these tales have themes closely related to nature; in "The Stone," for instance, the old man who in his youth could lift a huge rock now discovers, when in a moment of retrospection he attempts to return to his earlier years, that his strength has vanished, and an effort to raise the stone results in his collapse and death. The rock outlasts the farmer, and nature is thus viewed as more enduring and less tragic than man. In "The Stream" a portrait of an old hag is given. She had become demented sixty years previously when her husband of three days was accidentally killed while hunting. (Nature again destroys man, but implied is the suggestion that the woman should have adapted to life and nature by taking a new mate.)

Some of O'Flaherty's narratives are primarily descriptive documentaries. The most methodical and unimaginative but persevering reapers win in a contest for speed and thoroughness; impoverished tenants are evicted from their home; a bulky figure named Black Tom works off his frustrations in epic-style twice-a-year drinking bouts; a boy and his dog wantonly destroy a trapped rabbit; the terror and destruction which are constantly wrought by the sea—such is the typical subject matter with which the man of Aran is most comfortable.

Some of the stories are heavily Naturalistic in tone and descriptive detail. Thus, in a tale called "The Ditch" a grotesque-looking laborer rapes an ignorant, ugly farm girl. She bears her child in the most squalid circumstances possible and then goes berserk when she discovers that her lover has murdered the infant.

O'Flaherty's generally plain, flat, and rough style is especially noticeable in his short stories. Like Dreiser's writing, O'Flaherty's style usually appears to be laboring; it struggles; it is a sort of hewing-out-of-rock prose in which the hammering and the hard resistance of the words are apparent. The prose is undistinguished, and a decided preference for language that is hackneyed is evident. Clichés abound: "White—like the teeth of a Negro," "as quick as a cat," "pure like a young virgin," "he smiled like a happy child and his head swam." In O'Flaherty's superior stories, the clichés are fewer; the roughness blends well with the peasant and rural subject matter; and the earnest, accurate, detailed observation lifts the material to a more meaningful level of accomplishment and impact.

O'Flaherty's writing tone is generally bitter, grim, even sardonic. Rarely does he use humor; and, when he attempts comedy as, for example, in "The Stolen Ass," the humor is usually of the obvious tall-tale type. O'Flaherty also employs irony. In "A Red Petticoat"—a story which relates how an impoverished woman obtains credit at a grocery because she discovers that the proprietress is having an affair—the material becomes so stern and heavily ironic that very little comedy results. Such is usually the outcome of most of O'Flaherty's ironic efforts.

O'Flaherty, from time to time, makes use of satire to ridicule aspects of Irish life and behavior which he finds offensive. For example, he satirizes the clergy in several stories, as in "Offerings" and "The Strange Disease," and he attacks such abuses as profiteering and injustice on the part of storekeepers. But his satire possesses a gnarled heavy-handedness and is too pat and obvious didactic preachment to be successful. Indeed, the only effective satire O'Flaherty wrote in his career is "The Fairy Goose," which owes much of its felicitousness to a lightness achieved by the use of fantasy and colorful imagination. "The Fairy Goose" involves an odd-looking, strangely behaving gosling who is owned by an old woman named Mary Wiggins. When Mary comes to believe her pet to be a fairy, this idea is taken seriously in the village, and the strange gosling is regarded as sacred. Mary accepts commissions to unravel the meanings of dreams and to perform the ritual for spells.

The villagers agree that the goose is a beneficent spirit when a sickly cow is cured, allegedly through the influence of Mary Wiggins' pet.

Eventually, the local priest, informed of the situation, hastens in fury to Mary's house. He curses and terrifies her, the goose, and all those who believe in such superstition. When he preaches the fear of God, and his fumigations result in the death of the goose, Mary falls into a fit and places a curse on the village. Her curse appears to take effect since from that day on the people of the town become contentious drunkards who, although they fear God, hate one another. It is now remembered that this village had harmony only when the fairy goose was alive and was respected and loved by the people.

Allegorically, the fairy goose represents love; the parish priest, fear. The point of the allegory is rather blunted, however, because the foolishness of the fantasy—the behavior of the goose and the people, the silly decorations which embellish the goose, and other details—makes the concept so imaginatively playful and incredible that the harshness and the severity of the priest contrast not with reality but with a never-never story-book aura. O'Flaherty attempts to blend something essentially fantastical with realistic material, and the union of these two disparate elements, while effective enough as a mere story, does not make the allegorical point as convincing as it should be. O'Flaherty is condemning fear, religion, and the clerical elements associated with religion in Ireland. He is extolling love, which in the person of the goose is finally killed, but the apparatus in this story is too improbable to make the moral as meaningful as he intended.[11]

## II  *The Sketches of Animal Life*

While O'Flaherty was working on his first literary efforts in London in the early 1920's, Edward Garnett suggested that he return to Ireland and write about what he knew thoroughly.[12] When O'Flaherty protested that his most intensive knowledge was about cows, sea birds, and other animals, as well as native farming and fisher life, Garnett advised him to write about animals.[13] As a result, O'Flaherty began to produce countless animal-life sketches taken from firsthand observation. Thus O'Flaherty's finest early short stories are of two types: realistic portraits of aspects of life in rural Ireland—stories such as "Spring Sowing," "Going Into Exile," and "Red Barbara"—and some exceptionally striking animal vignettes.

Anyone living on the Aran Islands is especially conscious of animal life since, in addition to the domestic farm creatures, fish and birds are ubiquitous. Synge, when he visited Aran, was particularly surprised by the large variety of birds, by their "wild pastimes" on the cliffs, and by how the people became companions of "the cormorants and crows."[14] It is natural, therefore, that O'Flaherty should come to write about such familiar material. In most of his stories about animals, O'Flaherty aims to present as vividly as possible the physical aspects of some occurrence. The focus is, therefore, sharp and penetrating, direct, and essentially simple. Usually the subject is caught in a moment of conflict or during a time of tension so that the full emotional impact of the situation may impinge upon the reader with particular force. The scenes have the quality of a very detailed woodcut, for every line is immediately noticeable and meaningful. O'Flaherty once remarked to Frank O'Connor, "If you can describe a hen crossing a road you are a real writer."[15] This comment defines O'Flaherty's own approach to his stories: take very ordinary everyday scenes and attempt to describe these materials as concretely as possible.

"The Cow's Death" is typical of the animal sketches. The cow's appearance and reactions after having given birth to a stillborn calf are described so closely that the reader participates as an on-the-scene observer. As the cow's pain lessens and she cannot locate her calf (it has been taken away and thrown over a sea cliff to the rocks below), her every action is minutely catalogued. The author watches every reaction and photographs every occurrence. The cow's need for its offspring drives the animal to smell out the trail of bloodstains until it reaches the cliffs and sees the dead calf below. After endeavoring in every possible manner to reach the rocks on which the calf rests, the cow finally plunges over the cliff when she observes a large wave wash the calf away from the rocks.

Throughout the sketch O'Flaherty offers little in the way of comment. He is describing intimately in order that his reader may reflect on the fundamentals of birth, death, tragedy, mother love, pain, suffering, frustration. Nature, its conduct and characteristics, becomes the prime figure in the narrative. Both the writing and the scene have been reduced to bare, elemental facts, and the documentary bleakness builds up a compelling and penetrating chiaroscuro.

While "The Cow's Death" is characteristic of O'Flaherty's finest work in this form of story and has been a particular favorite of his,[16] several of the many other animal sketches are equally good. In "The Rockfish," for example, the description of the fisherman's bait and the conduct of the line as it sinks below the surface of the water is presented with marvelous exactitude. The reaction of the rockfish as they smell and dash about the bait is again presented with a camera eye. The individual reactions and varieties of movement are catalogued with the closest attention to completeness of detail. When a large rockfish does take the bait and is hauled up toward the fisherman, the struggles of the captured prey are sketched. As the tussle continues, the fish manages to tear a strip of his skin in which the hook is embedded. His continued gyrations enable him to break free although he loses part of the skin about his jaw.

O'Flaherty often conveys the element of chance involved in nature's activities. Some of the animals in his stories are unfortunate. They are killed or wounded by accident or because of the depredations of man or other animals. Other creatures, such as the rockfish, are more favored; they may be trapped, but they manage close escapes by the sheerest luck and continue their daily pursuits. No logic is involved in the selections between the fortunate and the unfortunate. Blind chance alone decides, for nature is indifferent.

Like the rockfish story, O'Flaherty's "The Conger Eel" offers another lucky creature of nature. While preying on a school of mackerel, the eel himself is accidentally caught in a fisherman's net. In his struggle to escape, he damages the net, but is caught more completely in its coils and is finally thoroughly enmeshed. When he is eventually hauled into the boat, the fishermen are irate because of the damage he has done to their net and because he has unintentionally helped many mackerel escape. After the fishermen free him from the net, their attempt to kill him is unsuccessful because he is too fast and elusive. The eel is finally grasped and lifted by the younger of the fishermen; but, before he can be killed, he slips free and falls into the sea, escaping to the depths of his lair.

Not so fortunate is the wounded cormorant in a story of that title. When a stone near the edge of the cliff of Clogher Mor is accidentally dislodged by a grazing goat, the rock missile crashes down on several cormorants who are resting on a large rock below the cliff. When the leg of one of the cormorants is broken by a stone that falls on top of him, the other cormorants immediately become hostile to their injured fellow. They attempt to keep the wounded one away from themselves and then fly off in an attempt to avoid its companionship. The wounded bird cannot fly well but does manage to reach his fellows when they settle on a ledge of the cliff. The other cormorants, however, are unwilling to allow their injured comrade to continue as a member of the flock. When the wounded cormorant comes to rest on the ledge with them, the others begin to attack him: "tearing at its body with their beaks, plucking out its black feathers and rooting it about with their feet. It struggled madly to creep in farther on the ledge, trying to get into a dark crevice in the cliff to hide, but they dragged it back again and pushed it towards the brink of the ledge. One bird prodded its right eye with its beak. Another gripped the broken leg firmly in its beak and tore at it." [17]

In time, the wounded cormorant no longer possesses the strength to endure the persistent onslaught of his fellows. He is forced off the edge of the ledge and falls into the water below. There a huge wave dashes the bird against the side of a jagged rock, and the wounded cormorant disappears into the seaweed strands below the water's surface. The cormorants have succeeded in killing their injured fellow; the savage instinct of the pack causes them to hound and bring a weaker member to doom.

Another phase of animal life is depicted in the equally vivid "Wild Goat's Kid." A wild goat who lives among the cliffs gives birth to a kid. While she goes out each day to forage, she always hides her offspring in a large crevice. Nevertheless, a wild dog manages to smell the presence of the young kid. He and the mother engage in a vicious fight, the mother to protect the life of her child, the dog to devour the kid and satisfy its hunger. The struggle between the two animals is described with incredible pictorial observation. O'Flaherty has obviously witnessed such a conflict; and the effect of his description is such that the scene could be no more completely captured or delineated. Every movement and every detail are recorded, and the whole episode rings with convincing authenticity.

"The Blackbird's Mate" also reflects the cruelty of nature. After the blackbird and his companion have mated, they enjoy their life together and the bounty of nature. Then they prepare a nest for the expected offspring. After a time, the hen bird produces four eggs. She sits on her nest, but cold and snow arrive in the area. The blackbird attempts to take his mate with him so that they can fly away to a sheltered location, but the mother refuses to leave the unhatched eggs. The snow prevents the birds from eating, and the intense cold is particularly harsh toward the mother bird. When the sun reappears after a few days and the snow begins to melt, the blackbird expresses his delight and pleasure. He immediately goes to seek food, but upon returning to the nest, he finds his mate dead from cold and hunger. The eggs, too, are cold and dead. The blackbird, bewildered, can only fly away and express his distress with a "piteous shriek." This narrative is another sketch about which, as Sean O'Faolain has observed, "one has the feeling that O'Flaherty has his ear to the earth, listening quietly." [18]

Some of O'Flaherty's other stories about animals which are exceedingly well delineated are: "His First Flight" (a young sea gull moves into the sky); "The Jealous Hens" (chickens torment a new hen until her owner is forced to give her to another farmer); "The Lost Thrush" (a baby thrush becomes separated from his parents); "Birth" (a calf is born, and the mother experiences love); and "The Wild Swan" (the swan's mate dies; the swan drives off a male, appropriates its mate, and the new couple prepare to propagate). All these sketches demonstrate O'Flaherty's gift in dramatizing the lives of animals and birds.

The most noticeable weakness found in some of these stories occurs when O'Flaherty fails to humanize the material. Some of these sketches are essentially description and nothing else, but others seek to enter "the blind, unreasoning life, the instincts, appetites, and terrors that lurk behind snout and beak and muzzle." [19] George Brandon Saul best describes this problem when he remarks that "the author's characteristic 'psychological' analyses of the behaviour and assumed mental processes of brute animals are more imaginative than persuasive, however accurate his reports of physical responses." [20] It is unquestionably true that O'Flaherty has periods of failure in trying to convey the thoughts or feelings of animal life, but he is more often successful than not. When a false note intrudes, it seems so possible and feasible that, in general, the questionable exaggerations and imaginative reflections are excusable in the light of the over-all effectiveness of the story.

All of O'Flaherty's animal sketches do not achieve the same height of artistry, but his best work in this form is unrivaled since he has observed his subjects so sensitively and so minutely and since he possesses a special gift for describing animal life. Frank O'Connor calls the animal sketches "masterly presentations of instinctual life." [21] These stories also demonstrate O'Flaherty's natural power of empathy; for, as Horace Reynolds notes, O'Flaherty has the gift to insert himself into "a man, a mouse, a wave" and to imagine with seeming accuracy how these particular objects feel. [22] H. E. Bates applauds the animal sketches for their "delicate feeling" and "visual brilliance." [23] And especially in portraying animal life, what was said by Edwin Muir of D. H. Lawrence can be applied also to O'Flaherty: "he has written in a new way . . . as if he were not their observer, but a mystical sharer in their being." [24]

O'Flaherty's short stories are usually rough-grained and unsophisticated, and the language is frequently flat and mechanical. It is also true that "O'Flaherty sometimes leaves us with the impression that his stories have either gone on too long or not long enough." [25] Furthermore, O'Flaherty is hampered by his story form; and O'Connor has best described the inherent weakness in this area: "In spite of the powerful narrative line, O'Flaherty's form is an art form, not a folk one; but it is the convenient, ready-to-wear magazine form of the Twenties—two or three thousand words describing a single episode—and while like the ready-to-wear suit it is a great convenience, the pattern is also in quantity very monotonous." [26]

A total picture develops, then, of a writer who has obvious faults and weaknesses but who, in his finest work, can write short narratives so "compact, so deeply felt, so instinctive . . . so surely conceived." [27] William Troy remarks that O'Flaherty as a short-story writer is "closer to the unknown writers of the early Gaelic folk literature than to any of his contemporaries," and is "less the product of any modern school than that of the period when European culture had not yet entirely lost its innocence." [28] This innocence and his "complete identification with nature" make O'Flaherty's best short stories—although limited in audience appeal by narrowness of range and subject—a refreshing, unique reading experience.

### CHAPTER 4

# *"Melodramas of the Soul"*

O N SEVERAL occasions, critics and reviewers have denigrated O'Flaherty for writing mere melodrama. His novels are heavily dependent on sensational elements, and his approach to his characters is intensely emotional. In 1929, William Troy, writing an analysis of O'Flaherty's work, defended O'Flaherty from critical attacks built on the charge of melodramatic. Troy initiated the description "melodrama of the soul," which has since furnished a convenient label for many of O'Flaherty's novels.

Melodrama in itself has been condemned as a literary mode because it usually exaggerates action and emotion beyond natural limits and results in falsification of life and people. Troy argues that a blanket censuring of melodrama is false and that such a condemnation of what may be called satisfactory melodrama "rests on a failure to determine the relationship between action and theme, on the failure to recognize that the treatment of certain themes requires the extension of action on a more strenuous and heroic plane than is normal." [1] Maintaining that *Macbeth* and *The Duchess of Malfi*, for example, are good melodramas, Troy argues that O'Flaherty's subject matter, which involves extremely emotional *dramatis personae* in situations of terror and flight, requires the melodramatic form. O'Flaherty's temperament, which has elements of emotional instability, plus his origins on the wild storm-swept Aran Islands, also add to his natural bent toward dealing with material in a melodramatic fashion.

In all O'Flaherty's early novels, melodrama is present; and the essential critical problem then becomes one of determining whether the characters and setting in a particular novel justify the melodramatic treatment. In *Thy Neighbour's Wife* and *The Black Soul* the excesses and the exaggerations of emotion frequently appear out of keeping with a logical and credible sense of probability. Too much "sound and fury" and too many variations and inconsistencies in presenting one sequence after another of emotional turmoil frequently render the novels artificial and untrue. On the other hand, *The Informer,* while possessing melodramatic aspects, is a much more satisfying and successful novel because the blending of character, subject matter, and emotional reaction is more logical and consistent.

O'Flaherty never eschews melodrama. He can never bring a Graham Greene sense of restraint when dealing with psychological probing in a context of highly charged emotional tension. But then, his characters, by temperament and by environment, are passionate types who wear their hearts on their sleeves. When an O'Flaherty novel fails, it does so primarily because the melodrama is not convincingly in keeping with the characterizations and the events which take place. Several of his novels are characterized by an unevenness in handling the melodramatic elements. Thus, parts of the books are excellently rendered and are persuasive and compelling while other sections are less credible and effective. Several critics have tended to neglect the successful aspects of O'Flaherty's novels and to denigrate his books on the basis of some of the ineffectual units and chapters. A more balanced approach to O'Flaherty's work, however, should place the strengths and weaknesses of his novels in a clearer light and demonstrate that the many successful aspects of his writing should not be ignored or glossed over by dismissing the books as mere melodrama. As Lillian Hellman once observed, "when violence is actually the needed stuff of the work and comes toward a large enough end, it has been and always will be in the good writer's field." [2] At O'Flaherty's best and in his most successful books, he generally uses melodramatic elements with both proper logic and for justifiable purposes and revelations.

## I   Mr. Gilhooley

One year after *The Informer* (1925), another O'Flaherty novel appeared which for a time seemed destined to rival the fame of O'Flaherty's most widely known novel. Indeed, in Ireland for a while, as Donagh MacDonagh observes, *Mr. Gilhooley* (1926) was as famous as Joyce's *Ulysses,*[3] and the Irish government even commissioned a stained glass representation of the title character which was to be given to the League of Nations building in Geneva.[4] William Butler Yeats called *Mr. Gilhooley* a "great novel," [5] and a further testimonial to the book's impact occurred when the story was adapted by Frank Elser and appeared as a Broadway play.[6] While over the years *Mr. Gilhooley* has faded in reputation, it deserves more respect than it presently receives; and the reasons for its popularity in the late 1920's and early 1930's are justified.

Lawrence Gilhooley, the novel's protagonist, is a forty-nine-year-old retired civil engineer. Gilhooley's heart has been injured while working in the high altitudes of the Andes; but after returning to Ireland for a brief period, his heart trouble ends. However, he does not wish to travel to South America again; and Ireland is not able to offer jobs suitable for his qualifications. Despite financial security, Gilhooley is now a lonely, extremely unhappy individual. A bachelor, living in a boardinghouse, he is beginning to be scarred by advancing age; and, unless some changes occur, he is likely to fall into a disorganized, old-before-his-time manner. Gilhooley passes his days with others who are roughly in the same predicament; and, "Like them, he became soured, disgruntled and miserable." [7] Especially touching is Gilhooley's reluctance to return to his lonely room. He will do almost anything to avoid this necessity. When he is forced to retire there for the night, he frequently does nothing for hours except sit in his bed, brooding on the emptiness of his life.

For several years he hopes for marriage, but he cannot find a suitable partner because he does not have the necessary family connections. Gradually his sensual nature forces him to mingle with prostitutes and other crude, tavern-oriented women who only increase his dissatisfaction and loneliness. He turns to heavy drinking and continues his bored, meaningless existence. It is apparent that Gilhooley is sinking to lower levels and that he may eventually become a candidate for skid row, although he still manages to cling to some gentility and outward propriety resulting from his temperament and his previous professional occupation.

One of Gilhooley's drinking companions maintains that there is divinity in everyone, but under the present circumstances much of Gilhooley's divinity is disappearing as he continues on his downward course. Gilhooley's future prospects are loneliness, increased bouts of drinking, and, finally, death: "No misery is as great as that of the lonely voluptuary who feels that his life is wrecked without any hope. Neither the misery of hunger, nor of homelessness, nor of disease. Because in all these miseries there is hope and a sense of righteousness. But in the misery of the bored voluptuary there is no hope nor sense of righteousness." [8] In his aloneness Mr. Gilhooley is reduced to touching an unknown lady's knee in the cinema; and, after a period of fright at the possibility of having this episode reach the newspapers, his fear departs and the shame overwhelms him—the shame that he has fallen to such a sad, pitiable level of conduct.

On occasion, Gilhooley, while intoxicated, revels in a state of maudlin self-pity. The emptiness of his days, "the hopelessness of his future, his solitude, the grossness of the set of imbeciles in which he moved," [9] and the sense of suffering bring him to sentimentality. Contrasts abound in the novel, and one of the earliest examples is the evaluation of the futility and meaninglessness of Gilhooley's present life with his dream of what life might have been—a productive existence as a farmer, having a wife and children, tilling the soil, raising livestock. Such a life would be of value, but his present circumstances persuade him that his life has been a complete waste.

In *Mr. Gilhooley,* as in some sections of other novels about Dublin life (for example, in his portrait of Connemara Maggie in *The Informer*), O'Flaherty presents existence in rural Ireland as the most desirable goal. The city is corrupt and contaminating; life on the farms or near the sea is purifying, for closeness to nature can inspire and elevate. Many Irish men and women, O'Flaherty indicates, wither when they are forced to leave their natural rural habitat. Such thoughts in O'Flaherty's writing, however, are generally sporadic and are never proclaimed as major themes; rather, they are bits of nostalgia and natural reflection resulting from a character's privations in the Dublin slums. In many of O'Flaherty's short stories and in such novels as *Thy Neighbour's Wife* and *The Black Soul,* the trials and difficulties of rural existence are too acutely revealed to persuade the close student of O'Flaherty's work that country life is especially preferable to dwelling in the city.

Larry Gilhooley toys with the notion of Arcadia, but his real vision of a utopian existence consists of love for a woman—not a mere sensual love but a pure, inspiring emotion treasured by every human being at least in the depths of his heart. With the peculiar timidity and puritanical attitudes toward love suffered by certain Irishmen—and Gilhooley is one such—love becomes an even grander ideal than it would ordinarily be.

When Gilhooley encounters Nelly Fitzpatrick, a young woman wandering about the streets, he assumes she is a prostitute although she bears no signs of that occupation. A homeless, waiflike creature, recently arrived in Dublin from Belfast, she is alone and hungry, and she arouses the lonely man's pity. Although he retains some suspicions, he treats her to a meal and promises her shelter for the night. When the owners of the lodging house discover that bachelor Gilhooley has brought a woman to his room, they evict him, and he and the girl are forced to seek other accommodations.

As their acquaintanceship develops, the character of the twenty-two-year-old Nelly takes on enigmatic qualities. She combines a basic youthful innocence with a hardened feminine subtlety that gradually increases in ruthlessness. When Gilhooley develops a sexual passion for her, the girl appears quite content to become his mistress and to allow him to support her, to buy her clothes, and to give her money. But no genuine understanding exists between them; they now share the plight of human beings "escaping from the consciousness of existence and the fear of death, through lust and drunkenness." [10]

As Gilhooley's passion for Nelly increases, so does his general emotional intensity. When he becomes jealous of another's attention to Nelly and causes an ugly quarrel and scene, Gilhooley is worried by his loss of control; he has intimations of more trouble—of disaster, of death. He begins to doubt the wisdom of his relationship with Nelly; but the alternative—his drinking companions (who once more appear on the scene), and his previous life of frightful isolation and emptiness—has no appeal. Gilhooley is at a crossroads: he can continue his relationship with Nelly despite his inklings of coming difficulties and his personal disintegration, or he can give up his involvement and his protector role and return to his former wretchedness.

During a brief encounter with his drinking companions, Gilhooley thinks of their recently expressed admiration for a gunman of the Irish Republican Army who had killed several people and who was revered by many of his countrymen. Gilhooley reflects about how he has never hurt nor killed anything in his life, not even a rabbit—and "yet nobody revered him, nobody had any interest in him, and if he died nobody" would really care. This thought is a convincing stimulus to make his decision easier, and he chooses the possibility of love with Nelly. He endeavors to establish a relationship in which his existence has some meaning not only to himself but also to someone else. He especially needs someone to care whether he lives or dies.

The appearance of Michael Friel, the house agent, serves to focus the story on two additional contrasts. Gilhooley believes that if he could marry his problems would be solved. He would be a loyal, devoted husband who would put nothing ahead of his relationship with his wife; he would not only give but receive warmth and tenderness. Friel, however, who proclaims how happily married he himself is, does not encourage Gilhooley or any of his acquaintances to marry. In fact, Friel, who practices promiscuity, recommends this way of life as more pleasurable and satisfying than faithfulness to one woman. Friel's youth also serves to remind Gilhooley of the fact that old age is quickly overtaking him and that, while Friel has all the time and youth to enjoy romantic affairs, he himself is nearing his last opportunity. Friel's thick, curly hair particularly absorbs Gilhooley's thought since he himself has a bald spot which he must carefully cover; and his meditations at this point run significantly: "If I only believed in God itself, it would be some comfort. She doesn't love me. I'm not a fool. Anything to fill a gap . . . provided there's money. He has black curls and he's young . . . same as I was once. . . . None of them believe me . . . Larry Gilhooley getting married! That baldy codger! Good for a loan and for a drink, that's all." [11] Although he realizes that Nelly does not love him, he must have her since she is all he can ever have.

In their new living quarters and immersed in the jolly celebration of a champagne supper, happiness and hope for the future become conceivable. Gilhooley is ecstatic: "his melancholy, his fear of the future and his disillusionment had vanished and . . . nothing was now required but generosity to unite this girl with him forever in love." [12] Hope is offered that he will receive needed sympathy and affection; but, at the same time, malignant fate, which is always in the background, and the sad, enigmatic look in Nelly's eyes, foretell that the elements of doom have gathered ominously about the lonely protagonist.

An Oedipal-like sense of unavoidable doom and disaster hangs over the novel. There are suggestions that Nelly is an evil spirit who will lure Gilhooley to destruction; she is called a Lorelei, a Duessa. When Gilhooley, thrilled by his contact with Nelly, repeats on several occasions, "I don't deserve this happiness," O'Flaherty underscores these statements with irony. Gilhooley attempts to put out of his mind "grinning" fate, which stands at a distance, associated with "imminent catastrophe." The image of malignant doom also recurs throughout in the phrase "the man with the club" who watches, broods, and symbolically pursues the protagonist. Finally, thoughts of the death of his father and his father's funeral are reiterated as symbols of the oppressive destruction and tragedy which pervade the book. Gilhooley has been marked by the fates for a generally unfortunate life and death.

Disillusionment again appears when Gilhooley discovers that Nelly is writing to Matt Considine, her former lover. She justifies her behavior by insisting that her relationship with Gilhooley is strictly a business matter, for she openly admits that she does not care for her middle-aged protector, and refuses to accept seriously the fact that Gilhooley is in love with her, wants to marry, and settle down.

Nelly Fitzpatrick's conduct and attitude are governed by her half-love, half-hate attitude toward Considine. Suggestions of Matt Considine loom continually in the background as she constantly attempts to persuade herself that Matt will return and claim her. When she has sexual intercourse with Gilhooley, she frequently pretends that she is with Matt. Although she has ample evidence to convince her that Matt is no longer interested, she cannot give him up, and, even when she learns he has married and emigrated to Canada, she still will not completely accept the termination of their love affair: she considers pursuing him to America to regain his attention. In her reveries, she veers from love and hope to hate and despair. She half-realizes that Matt is lost to her but can never fully admit this fact. She is so emotionally involved with Considine that any other man can only be a substitute. She is really a child, behaving in a purely unstable, emotional manner because of her attachment to Considine.

Violently agitated by Nelly's attitude, Gilhooley becomes more and more confused in thought and behavior. He is frustrated and enraged. He now realizes that he can never have his love satisfied, and this thought unbalances him. He proclaims that he loves Nelly and that he could not now allow her to go with either Friel or Considine. Mental derangement continues to increase, and near the end of the novel he strangles Nelly while she holds a picture of Considine to her bosom. During his act of murder Gilhooley is not really conscious of what he is doing. His intense jealousy--the primal cause of his irrational behavior (foreshadowed earlier by a wild, frightening encounter with another lodger, by his mental rages, and his attempt to procure a gun)—makes him the victim of interior forces.

Only later, after many hours have passed, does Gilhooley realize that he has killed the only one he has ever loved in order to prevent her from leaving him. As he wanders in a daze about Dublin, he seeks some meaning for his life and for existence in general. Searching the heavens, he can find no God. He is left with the "universal emptiness" of earth and of life. His anguish and despair result in suicide.

In analysis, Mr. Gilhooley's character can be seen in all its manifestations, and the portrait is one of validity. O'Flaherty has captured the pervasive bitterness and misery of a lonely, middle-aged man with moving empathy; the frightful isolation of life; a last hope for love and some meaning; and the concomitant failure, frustration, and then madness—all are realized so well because O'Flaherty has projected himself so thoroughly into Gilhooley. No false romantic excess mars Gilhooley's portrait as is the case with the protagonists in O'Flaherty's first two novels. What O'Flaherty has done so convincingly is to dissect a lonely, searching soul who would, if Nelly had not appeared, have ended his days on the verge—at the very least—of a Bowery-type existence. The particular isolation of the unloved reaches forth with considerable emotion and, with the realization that Gilhooley's drinking companions want only whatever money he can loan them and not his company, brings the book to a universal level of pathos, explaining almost too much about people and loneliness. O'Flaherty's accomplishment in delineating the Gilhooley type makes this novel one of his finest books.

Nevertheless, the novel has two weaknesses. First, when O'Flaherty is describing Gilhooley's growing disintegration after the revelation about Nelly's attachment to Considine and her interest in Friel, he does not convey the protagonist's emotional turmoil as convincingly as possible. Although the situation warrants intense emotion, O'Flaherty appears to carry this material beyond the bounds of belief. Gilhooley's emotional stress is not only overworked but is sketched too quickly, with only a few essentially repetitive and circular notes. When the reader should receive a more gradual and a more penetrating Dostoevski-like probing, O'Flaherty's handling of the distraught Gilhooley lacks the necessary profundity and careful internal revelation of psychological processes at work which are needed to tone down the melodramatic simplicities. Gilhooley's behavior is not illogical, but O'Flaherty's handling of Gilhooley in the last third of the novel lacks both a needed delicate restraint and a persuasive complexity.

A more serious defect in this particular narrative is the characterization of Nelly. Her initial introduction in the book causes confusion because we are first led to believe that she is a sweet, innocent child. Our credulity is strained by being forced to accept the premise that such a starving, shabbily dressed, and seemingly innocent waif could be wandering alone through the streets of Dublin. While Gilhooley is a twentieth-century figure, Nelly at first appears to be a character out of a fairy tale who is at first partly Cinderella and partly Little Nell. For a while, as she lives with Gilhooley, she is able to maintain a certain sense of cuddly innocence. On the basis of the background suggestions of malignant fate and oncoming doom, it is apparent that the Gilhooley-Nelly relationship will end unhappily; but, for a while, faith in Nelly herself is retained.

Not until almost two-thirds of the novel has passed does Nelly show an unsavory viciousness. Her callousness toward Gilhooley; her business-like "I'll give you a good time, provided you give me a good time"; and her conduct with Friel display another side of her. Although fictional logic demands foreshadowing earlier in the novel of such traits, such suggestions of imperfections in Nelly's character are relatively slight and secondary; and she certainly does not appear to be as hard, tough, violent, and unlikable as she is later in the book. It may be argued that if Nelly had revealed these serious blemishes sooner, Gilhooley would not have been attracted to her. But O'Flaherty could have presented her character in such a manner as to make her shift from a pseudo-innocence to viciousness less abrupt and hence more persuasive. When, in the last third of the novel, Nelly's character is completely revealed, she is a realized human being; and if the reader had known earlier that Nelly simply wanted a temporary substitute for Matt Considine, an even deeper feeling for Gilhooley would have been developed, and Nelly's character would be more understandable and no later jarring would occur.

That O'Flaherty himself may have belatedly realized that his treatment of Nelly was not so sure-handed as it could have been is indicated by some of the textual changes made after the first British edition of the book was published. In later English and all American editions of *Mr. Gilhooley,* most of the textual changes render Nelly a more ladylike character; and, since these changes occur in the last third of the ·book, it appears that O'Flaherty is softening the delineation of his heroine rather than just endeavoring to avoid censorship. In one place, for example, "bitch" is changed to "filly," [13] and on three other occasions the word "bitch" used to describe Nelly is omitted altogether,[14] while the phrase "whore of a story" in a passage relating to some of Nelly's activities is altered to read "whale of a story."[15]

But even these changes do not succeed in making Nelly's character more convincing. Obviously, O'Flaherty does not wish to paint Nelly in unduly harsh colors; he wants us to understand her and also to sympathize with her plight. She has been reared in a workhouse because she has no parents or relatives to guide her. After this unhappy childhood, she has then fallen in love with young and handsome Matt Considine. The great love of her life, he has furnished her an opportunity for the kind of passion a girl feels when she is young. When Considine eventually has rejected her, she has been shattered; and she has turned to Gilhooley because she has needed food and shelter and has wanted to mark time while finding a way to renew Considine's interest. Sunk in her selfishness, she has never really understood Gilhooley or his need and genuine affection for her. This blind, selfish preoccupation is her limitation, but in O'Flaherty's view she is not to be condemned for this attitude. This is simply the way things have turned out; this is the way things are. Gilhooley's dreams of an ideal love are thwarted by the inherent defects of life, by the domination of human nature's sensuality, which, in O'Flaherty's view, man cannot control or master with rationality or common sense.

The way the book works itself out, however, Gilhooley as the salient figure is so well drawn that he arouses the principal attention as well as sympathy for his lonely anguish. Nelly, much less credibly manipulated, appears, as a result, to be an unmitigated villainess when, in actuality, O'Flaherty means her to be another unfortunate victim of life. Furthermore, a strong misogynist element appears in O'Flaherty's makeup. His descriptions of several of the women in *The Informer* and particularly his description of a Dublin street prostitute in *Mr. Gilhooley*, followed by the hero's vehement denunciation of women as a group, are just a few illustrations of a recurring disillusionment and negativism. Some of this misogyny is unfortunately allowed to enter the portrait of Nelly.[16]

Truly, however, *Mr. Gilhooley* is one of the most compelling and heartrending studies of the lonely middle-aged man ever rendered in fiction. The intense loneliness and emptiness of existence without meaning or love is realistically translated to a visualization and even a figurative tasting of the situation that are genuinely affecting. Yet the novel would have been even more successful if its author had been as adept at handling women characters as he is at understanding his male figures.

## II   The Assassin

In O'Flaherty's next novel, *The Assassin* (1928), he continues to concentrate his main attention on the behavior and the psychological states of characters who labor under particularly great emotional stress and anguish. This novel takes its origin from the assassination of Kevin O'Higgins, vice president of the Executive Council and minister of justice and external affairs in the Free State government, who was murdered in 1927, supposedly by Irish Republican Army opponents.[17] Michael McDara, the chief conspirator in the book, has plotted a political murder for three years; the assassination of an important government figure has been his principal thought during this whole period. McDara, who had fought for the rebels in Ireland and who had escaped from an internment camp, has thus been subject to the pressures and strains of warfare, imprisonment, and obsession with assassination.

The time, the years after the Civil War when the Free State forces have overwhelmed the Republicans, is not propitious to rebel activity. The Irish Republican Army remnants are scattered, disorganized, disillusioned, and apathetic. The country is filled with spies who are ready to report any suspicious activity. Into this situation comes McDara, fresh from three years' refuge in the United States. He establishes himself in Dublin in the most inconspicuous manner possible and moves about stealthily. He maneuvers and plans with a vast amount of cunning. Although excessively excitable qualities are observed in McDara, his early plans and movements indicate a bold, callous nature perfectly adapted to the contemplated mission.

In order to carry out his plot, McDara requires the assistance of a few supporters; but the motives of these revolutionaries differ from his. His associates, who hope to stir up the people to another rebellion, expect that the populace will be so aroused by the killing that a fresh upheaval will occur: "In twenty-four hours after the job is done this town is goin' to be in the middle of a revolution." After the planned assassination is completed and a mob is stirred up, McDara's allies suggest that they then should assassinate a prominent Irish Republican Army figure. This act will seem to be a reprisal and will create more turmoil. General chaos is expected as a consequence: "Man, man, there are thousands waiting ready to rush out, waitin' for their chance." Such a development repels McDara because he regards it, in part, as mob anarchy. Above all, McDara is not desirous of supporting such activities because he no longer believes in the people, and he does not now care whether they rise and overthrow the present Free State government. His motive is entirely personal: he wishes to perform what he regards as a courageous act which would give his life new meaning and justify his existence.

But, as his planning and preparations continue, McDara becomes more dubious about the heroic nature of his intentions and more skeptical about the meaning of life. He remarks to Kitty Mellett, the courier:

I have now reached the climax of my dream. I expected to find here a new relevation of life and an explanation of the purpose of my existence. Instead I find myself in a slum, in a dirty room, in darkness, with two trivial fellows, who have nothing in common with me. I am going to do something which had [sic] no meaning and is simply waste of energy. I know that and yet I am going to do it, although it means nothing and it will have no effect, neither for the purpose of explaining my life nor for any other purpose. The whole thing is futile and a gross waste of energy. These men are childish brutes and I also am a childish brute, without any power. So! Well, then! So that is what life is. A childish farce. Ten million ants are not as great as one lion, although they make cities and obey their laws.[18]

The assassination is carried out, however, with great efficiency. Timothy McShiel, a prominent member of the Free State government group, is gunned down by McDara and his associates; and, for a while, McDara exults in his success. In a short time, however, weariness and depression engulf him. He recalls his childhood and imagines himself calling for his mother's assistance. When she does not respond to his cries, he becomes aware of the present moment and of the fact that his mother, being dead, cannot help him. Loneliness is now the supreme obsession. For the first time, he fully realizes that he is now truly isolated, that he has no meaningful contact with other human beings. When he imagines being hanged for his crime, he thinks of being taken to a scaffold in the cold of dawn and feels the noose tighten about his neck in a meditation that is associated with a vision of his childhood during which he unsuccessfully attempted to engage his mother's attention. Innocence has been lost along with the beliefs he once held in his fellow man and in God. His feeling of apartness increases, and his separate and aloof "state of inhumanity" becomes pervasive. Escape from Ireland only serves to reinforce his despondency; he is now an outcast from his native land and must continue to wander in perpetual loneliness. Suicide becomes the only means to ease the hopelessness of his existence and the nihilism of his thoughts.

*The Assassin* is a novel which could easily be subtitled "O'Flaherty at his best and at his worst." This book, which follows in the vein of *The Informer* rather than in the more florid and flaccid poetic exuberance of *The Black Soul,* makes effective use of all the storytelling tricks of plot suspense and tension. The author details McDara's preparations for the assassination with meticulous credibility and grippingly carries the reader through the various tensions and doubts suffered by the plotters. The act of assassination itself and McDara's escape to England are artistically wrought in the best thriller tradition.[19] The same absorbing, narrative-yarn excitement demonstrated in *The Informer* is handled again with the raw talent of the born storyteller.

Apart from its interest as an interesting and well-told story, *The Assassin* must succeed or fail on the effectiveness of O'Flaherty's

psychological analysis of McDara. The other revolutionaries have a
credible purpose for their activity. McDara, however, remains un-
acceptable as a character simply because his creator has not made his
purposes and his conduct believable. For a man who accepts nothing, it
is difficult to understand—at least from O'Flaherty's handling—why
McDara goes to such trouble to kill McShiel. McDara is not motivated
by revenge, by political dogma, by philosophic anarchism, or by any of
the other elements which might help to make his conduct more
understandable.

Obviously, McDara is supposed to derive a raison d'être from a
cold-blooded act of assassination. In a sense, he is a derivative of
Dostoevski's Raskolnikov who intends to achieve a notion of personal
power and meaning from an act of violence. But, since McDara himself
is muddled and uncertain about this point, his character becomes
enigmatic. He could perhaps be accepted as a madman if his general
conduct and behavior did not appear so relatively logical and
reasonably thought out. The root of the difficulty is O'Flaherty's
failure to analyze McDara in a satisfactory manner. O'Flaherty himself
seems to be uncertain of how to explain McDara; and he, therefore,
makes a halfhearted attempt to do so. Despite much potential, the
novel is a failure because of this central artistic weakness; and no
amount of clever, suspenseful storytelling can hide or overshadow this
basic defect.

A suspicion arises that, instead of taking care, time, and patience in
developing the characterization of McDara, O'Flaherty has slurred over
the matter as hastily and as superficially as possible. This feeling derives
from not only the unsatisfactory analysis of McDara but also from
O'Flaherty's rather unique dedication of this book: "To My Creditors,"
an assertion which is certainly to be taken ironically as well as literally.
This point raises the crucial question of O'Flaherty's writing for money.
It has been maintained by more than one critic that too much of
O'Flaherty's work has been produced for frankly commercial
reasons,[20] and this charge is not without supporting evidence.

In describing the composition of one of his books, O'Flaherty said at
one point that he "no longer wrote for the love of writing, of pouring
out words and gambolling among the fantastic creatures of my
imagination. I wanted to finish a novel, to sell it for money and free
myself from these two women [patrons at that time]. And this sordid
motive robbed the work of all pleasure."[21] Yet on another occasion,
while under the influence of Edward Garnett, he reminisces that
"Artistic beauty being the only thing of real importance in life to him, I

became a fervent disciple of that religion. I abandoned at once all thought of making a 'success' in life, of gaining fame or money." [22]

After making this comment, O'Flaherty soon launches into a discussion of the general public's failure to support artists. Among other examples he cites the case of Mary Webb, who he insists had died because the reading public had allowed her to starve. He spoke of his readers in the following manner: "Considering that I have always treated [the reading public] with the contempt which it deserves, it has been immoderately kind to me. After the first ecstasy of being able to express my ideas in writing had given way to a calculated scheme for making money out of writing, I cast about for a trick that would draw the attention of the public." [23] He then proceeds to claim that with this strategy he produced *The Informer*[24] and that he wrote this book with tongue in cheek. This comment, made in *Shame the Devil*, not only confuses the issue but must be taken *cum grano salis* when we read later in the same book that "Even my confessions were hypocrisy, for they were made in arrogance, as by one who wishes to make plain to all men that he can go naked without fear of mankind's mud staining his nakedness." [25]

The confusion in attempting to settle O'Flaherty's attitude toward writing as art and writing as a source of financial advancement persists throughout his career. In December, 1927, he proclaims in *The Irish Statesman:* "I don't write for money. If I wanted to write for money I could be a rich man now." [26] He insists that he writes only to please himself, his wife, and Edward Garnett.[27] In his autobiographical-travel volume, *I Went to Russia,* he informs his readers that he is writing this book for money; but then launches into a diatribe against democracy and the machine for having made literature into an industry rather than an art. Writers, O'Flaherty argues, must now write for the particular tastes of the reading public. At the moment (1930–1931), O'Flaherty maintains that two types of books are fashionable: autobiographies and works about the Bolsheviks. O'Flaherty claims that he was forced by hunger to write an autobiography (*Two Years,* 1930), and now he is required by economic necessity to write about the Russians. He asserts: "I write it [his book about Russia] honestly, for the sole purpose of making some money." [28]

Exactly forty pages later, he remarks: "I tried to tell myself that I had set out on this journey, not only for the trifling purpose of writing a book and earning some money, but also, with the more important idea of finding a new purpose in life, something to which I could attach myself." [29] This inconsistency is typical of O'Flaherty's nonfictional statements. He makes wild declarations, later contradicts or qualifies them, and then continues the same procedure for page after page. Since his makeup is governed by the emotion or mood of the moment, he jots down the immediate feeling. A little later, when the day is brighter and the mood has changed, the opposite feeling is recorded—and so on back and forth, regardless of the over-all contradictory impressions given.

It should be noted, of course, that such contradictions are not restricted to pronouncements on money matters. In *Shame the Devil,* for example, he professes his "one virtue, that I do love humanity." [30] In *I Went to Russia* he asserts, "I loathe the multitude, except as a spectacle to be watched, an ant-hill on the march." [31] This vacillation between love and hatred for the ordinary man is constant throughout much of his writing. Other issues receive similar treatment. O'Flaherty's comment after rereading one of his own books is particularly apropos of his chameleon-like attitudes: "It is the most inconsistent book I ever read. The man who wrote it, or rather the spirit that wrote it, must be as changeable as a weather-cock in an uncertain wind." [32] Such an inconsistent attitude also helps to mar O'Flaherty's portraits of Nelly in *Mr. Gilhooley* and McDara in *The Assassin.*

Probably the best insight (although partly unintentional) O'Flaherty has given in regard to his attitude toward money occurs in the following passage:

It was only natural for a man of my temperament, let loose with a sum of money (even though it was a small sum), to forget the future as long as he had the means of enjoying its pleasures. By nature I find real pleasure only in thought and in the observation of life. . . . While I have money I cease to concern myself with earning more until I have spent what I have. Because I carry the home of my ambition within me and not without as other men conceive it, enclosed within walls, with wives, children, social position, wealth of all kinds, I am unhappy only when I am forced by the encroachments of society to change my course from the limitless circuit of my brooding. Even now when I am weaving tales, a business most suited to my nature, I am unhappy because I have to sell them in order to buy leisure for weaving more. I have sometimes to think of the future. [33]

It appears, then, that O'Flaherty's temperament is such that, left to himself, he would have written perhaps eight or nine books; but, spurred by financial necessity, O'Flaherty wrote several books, such as the feeble potboiler, *The Return of the Brute,* [34] the melodramatic and overplotted *House of Gold,* and the hopelessly inadequate *Hollywood Cemetery.* He also produced several other works which are mixed in result because parts are distinguished by his storytelling ability but are marred by excessively hasty composition and by a failure to think out and develop adequately all the ramifications of character. *The Assassin* is one such book. It does not possess the over-all impact and effectiveness of *The Informer* and *Mr. Gilhooley,* and it shares with *Mr. Gilhooley* inadequate character portraiture in the cases of Nelly and McDara. But it demonstrates enough talent to make us wish that O'Flaherty had not allowed a certain natural inertia in his nature to combine with immediate economic need and, hence, produce a work which, while well done in parts, lacks consistency and logic in characterization.

### III   The Puritan

In studying the protagonist of *The Puritan,* O'Flaherty offers one of his most interesting excursions into psychological analysis.[35] Francis Ferriter, unquestionably the most self-torturing and tormented hero in a long list of such typically O'Flaherty characters, is a Catholic religious fanatic during the post-Civil War period in Ireland in the late 1920's and early 1930's—historically an era when religious conservatism and puritanism were thriving. Ferriter had participated in religious vigilante group actions such as book burnings, and he was extremely satisfied when the DeValera government in 1929 succeeded in passing the Censorship Act against the sale of allegedly immoral books.[36] In addition to being a psychoanalytic study of one figure, the novel is also an attempt to demonstrate the horror of modern Irish puritanism and in O'Flaherty's own words, "the Fascist tendency to regimentation which is characteristic of puritanism." [37]

To an extremist like Ferriter, it appears that the whole of Ireland is wallowing in evil of one sort or another, while only a few dedicated and holy individuals such as himself are maintaining the necessary proper standards of spiritual perfection and idealism. In the light of his convictions and sense of righteousness, Ferriter is capable of any conduct since he believes that all his activities are vindicated by God and the Catholic religion. When he puts "For the Greater Honor and Glory of God" stamp on his actions, he can convince himself that any of his deeds are justified. He regards himself as a crusader for the proper maintenance of religious and civic duty and behavior; and, if necessary, he intends to be an avenger of unlawful conduct.

Carrying out his conviction that he is a vigilante, a ferret of evil, and a divinely chosen moral avenger, the twenty-four-year-old Ferriter murders Teresa Burke, a prostitute who lives in his apartment building. Ferriter regards his deed as an act of blood sacrifice. Since, in his view, Teresa has become a symbol of impurity because of her sexual promiscuity, Ferriter believes that her death serves as a moral purification; it will help the world "be washed clean of sin in the blood of a harlot." The murder of Teresa is also supposed to punish those who were not living in the rigorous manner that Ferriter's notion of religion prescribes. Furthermore, he wishes to "rouse the country to a holy war against immorality. Had he not seen himself as the leader of this holy war while the divine fire of fanaticism was preparing him to commit the murder?"[38]

Although Ferriter is a violently excitable individual who engages in furious rages, he cannot commit murder without a justifiable (to his mind) motive. He can kill only under the banner of what he regards as some kind of acceptable purpose. For example, when he thinks of killing Corish, the newspaper editor who fires him, he doubts that such a murder could be an act of blood sacrifice; consequently, he is immediately repelled by the thought.

Ferriter even goes to the point of devising a written proclamation declaring his pseudo-philosophical viewpoint. The contents of Ferriter's manifesto are characteristic of the man. He believes that the world is being overwhelmed by the forces of Antichrist. He readily cites the oppression of religion in Mexico, Russia, and Spain to support his point; and he maintains that, when open persecution of religion is not in effect, subversion is in operation. Satan is using materialistic greed and lust to lure humanity away from the highest pursuits. Ferriter is convinced that many Christians are either complacent about the menace involved, or else they are involved by co-operating in one way or another with materialism and sexual impurity. His documentary call rises in crescendo:

Fellow soldiers of Christ, we must make another sacrifice of blood. This is necessary, just as the sacrifice of Calvary was necessary, in order to give us a fresh realization of man's purpose on this earth. A violent shock is necessary to show us the horror of our sins, just as the burning of Sodom and Gomorrah was necessary. . . . [There must be] a violent expression of the anger of the faithful. Sinners must be struck down in death, so that we may be redeemed by their blood. We must purify ourselves by pouring out the blood of sinners. We must put an end to sin and corruption by this sacrifice. Too long have the just been sacrificed on the altar of Mammon. Now the sacrifice must be the blood of the agents of Antichrist. . . .[39]

After the murder of Teresa Burke is committed and Ferriter observes the horrified reaction of other Dubliners, he begins to doubt his mission. He notices that in addition to the general public's repulsion, they regard the victim with sympathy. When some suspicion falls upon him, his fear of being convicted and executed for the crime intensifies his feelings of doubt and worry about the wisdom of his act. He begins to brood and wonder if his act of alleged blood sacrifice came from an evil source within him rather than originated from the purest of motives.

He is especially critical of those people and groups in the nation who, he feels, should, on the basis of their beliefs, support him: extremist clergymen and fanatic religious laymen who have created intolerance and a form of inquisitional approach to matters of supposed immorality. It is true that these individuals—at least knowingly—in this time and place would probably not advocate murder; yet, in a sense, Ferriter has carried their attitudes and preachments to a logical consequence. In some cases, murder has been recommended, however, by the wildest extremists. For example, a writer for one of the religious publications, a publication later suspended by the archbishop, and a schoolmaster named Brabazon had stressed the notion of religious assassination. At first, Ferriter had rejected this concept because he objected to the idea of shedding blood. (Brabazon had proposed that he and Ferriter should kill a writer who had written what many people considered an obscene book.) Later the notion grew more acceptable, and Ferriter sympathized with the killings of various government officials in Mexico who were persecuting religion.

By committing murder, Ferriter has reduced the hypothetical abstractions of such as Brabazon to the concrete. When Ferriter's act of murder does not receive the approval of these fanatical elements, he realizes more completely that his deed was not what he had conceived it to be; and he comes to understand that the religious zealots with the book-burning mentality are false and vile. When Ferriter learns that such individuals and organizations are petty, vicious, and hypocritical, this knowledge is too late to help him behave rationally. Ferriter becomes aware of the fact that such groups are usurping the activities or prerogatives of the police so that they can exalt themselves as being especially religious and virtuous.

As a consequence, Ferriter experiences a vehement reversal of viewpoint, and he angrily denounces a priest in the confessional and leaves the church because it can offer him no comfort. Later, when he is traveling from tavern to tavern and is escorted by three ersatz Furies in a seamy section of the city, he rejects his previous position of religious fanaticism.

In order to explain Ferriter's character in more detail, O'Flaherty traces his personality and development. O'Flaherty stresses that the novel's protagonist has suffered all his life from poor health. He had felt this difficulty especially in school when he had been unable to do the work of which he had believed himself capable. He had also been unhappy because he had not been accepted by his classmates who had teased him and made him the victim of numerous pranks. He has had no close associates and, therefore, has brooded upon his troubles and has become more disturbed.

Despite these drawbacks, Ferriter has always desired to be a genius. He has wanted favorable attention, and he has been vitally concerned with doing something newsworthy and sensational. The desire to perform some act which would "astonish humanity" has become an obsession. When he ultimately confesses to the murder of the prostitute, Ferriter seems to believe that this need to attract notice is really the primary motive which has goaded him into action.

Ferriter wrestles with his motives as guilt increases and torments him. He also claims that he killed Teresa in order to determine if there is a God and if man has a divine destiny. If, according to Ferriter's manner of thinking, man has a divine goal, then evil must be eliminated, since otherwise evil would overwhelm mankind and prevent humanity from reaching its destined end.

As Ferriter continues to torment himself, his sensitivity, his highly emotional nature, and the activity of his conscience bring him more to the realization that jealousy is a basic motive of his crime. Ferriter comes to admit that he had loved Teresa and to realize that she had had no interest in him and had devoted her attention to Dr. Michael O'Leary, a handsome playboy physician who was her lover. Ferriter also has developed an intense hatred for O'Leary, and he has condemned him as a brutish sensualist, lacking sensitivity and refinement. Yet, on the other hand, he has envied O'Leary's power to attract women and attention by wild behavior and debaucheries. He has wished to kill the physician, but he has not possessed enough courage to attempt such an act because of O'Leary's powerful build and violent temper. Readers of *The Puritan* are left to reflect that the motives for Ferriter's crime were various and intermingled. It would appear, however, that he has been moved chiefly by thwarted love and jealousy.

In the maniacal condition he reaches at the end of the novel, Ferriter feels triumphant because he insists that by his actions he has made a significant revolt and he has proved to his own satisfaction that "There is no God, but man has a divine destiny. It is the duty of each man to become God." [40] Although he pays for his exaltation and achievement by ultimate insanity and death, Ferriter has been, in his way, a spirit out of the ordinary, a spirit shouting defiance at the heavens. In one of his autobiographical commentaries, O'Flaherty declared: "I am convinced that the divinity in man's destiny is his struggle towards the perfection of his species to a state of godliness, and that the most perfect types of manhood are always in revolt against the limitations of man's nature, his position on the face of the earth, and his ignorance." [41] After Ferriter's repudiation of his fanaticism, he becomes a hero—in the eyes of O'Flaherty—because he pursues man's divine destiny. However, danger always resides in a man's concept of himself as being God—or in his taking unto himself the rendering of God's justice.

Several units in *The Puritan* are modeled on material used by Dostoevski in *Crime and Punishment*. Ferriter's act of bloody murder in the woman's apartment, the numerous intermingled motives which brought him to commit the crime, the cat-and-mouse game played with Police Superintendent John Lavan—these and similar elements have their origin in Dostoevski; but again a comparison with the Russian novelist does not work in O'Flaherty's favor. O'Flaherty's writings lack the depth, completeness, and intensity found in Dostoevski's work.

O'Flaherty delighted in the "brooding maniacs" of Dostoevski; he was pleased with the Russian's ability to depict "all the slovenliness, the insanity, the poverty, the melancholy, the wild passions that goaded people, forcing them to rise up and escape from the tortures of incomprehensible immensity by the performance of some wild feat." [42] Since Dostoevski's "desolate characters" were always capable of some "wild feat of genius," they particularly appealed to O'Flaherty because, as Benedict Kiely observes, the reckless, violent gesture deeply appealed to O'Flaherty's romantic soul. "Dignified by that gesture, even the troglodytes of the Dublin slums, as O'Flaherty sees them, can for moments be worthy of the earth on which they move." [43]

In another commentary O'Flaherty remarks: "As he spoke he [the captain of the ship taking O'Flaherty to Russia] almost lashed himself into a state of frenzy, so that I could hear the ghoulish characters of Dostoevski thrusting themselves forward from between his teeth, the Karamazovs, the Idiots, the Devils and the strange creatures from the House of the Dead, wild and wonderful geniuses, ashamed of their barbaric ancestors, clawing greedily at all the beautiful philosophies of

Europe, to use as tools for paring off their savage humps and warts."[44]
Although the affinities between Dostoevski's characters and
O'Flaherty's are clear, and although O'Flaherty has often transposed his
scenes and figures from Russia to Ireland, the Irish writer has not been
able—except in *The Informer, Mr. Gilhooley,* and *Skerrett,* and
sporadically in some of the other novels—to make his brooding and
desolate maniacs as credible, as developed, and as fascinating as their
counterparts in Dostoevski's books.[45] Dostoevski does not feel more
deeply than O'Flaherty, but he can transmit a greater power and
intensity, so that when "the slovenliness, the insanity, the poverty, the
melancholy, the wild passions that goaded people" are presented in
Dostoevski's work they are conveyed with more penetration and with
greater credibility. Dostoevski can carry such elements to the nth
degree, one hundred percent; O'Flaherty reaches about a sixty percent
level.

O'Flaherty not only lacks Dostoevski's patience and his detailed
knowledge of psychology, he is also hampered by his desire for haste.
He sketches the basic points or writes a neat outline. Dostoevski
elaborates on the basic points and fills in and develops the minor
headings in the outline. Even when O'Flaherty attempts to elaborate in
more complete detail, he is still impatient to get on with his narrative,
to furnish the answers in a less complex and, at times, oversimplified
manner. Ferriter, for example, has just as many motives for murder as
Raskolnikov has; but, because of Dostoevski's greater thoroughness and
massive analysis, Raskolnikov becomes much more memorable and
three-dimensional.

To make this comparison is not to indicate, however, that Ferriter is
a character easily forgotten or that *The Puritan* is insignificant. The
book possesses many vivid episodes (for example, the wild scene in the
confessional—when Ferriter, goaded into a frenzy, because the clergyman refuses to condone murder, spits in the priest's face, and threatens
to kill him—is handled most believably); and the hero's torments and
anguish are impossible to erase. But, in comparison to the best books
produced by O'Flaherty's *maître, The Puritan* does not reach the same
plateau of accomplishment.

## IV   Skerrett

Although *Skerrett* (1932) has been labeled one of O'Flaherty's finest
novels by several critics,[46] it would be more accurate to remark that
the book fails to be great although seeds of greatness are present. In

relating the story of David Skerrett, a schoolmaster who at the age of thirty-five goes to one of the desolate Aran islands to bring knowledge and enlightenment, O'Flaherty intends to exalt a man of essential nobility who emphasizes the things of spirit. O'Flaherty concludes the novel with these words: "the nobility of Skerrett's nature lay in his pursuit of godliness. He aimed at being a man who owns no master. And such men, though doomed to destruction by the timid herd, grow after death to the full proportion of their greatness." [47]

O'Flaherty's purpose embraces a contrast between Skerrett and Father Moclair, the wily and powerful parish priest of the island of Nara. Although Moclair triumphs during his lifetime, we are informed by the author that, after Moclair's death, the priest's reputation declines because "Moclair's virtues were of the body, allied to the cunning which ministers to the temporal body's wants, so do they wither quickly into nothingness." [48] The portrait of Moclair is consistent with O'Flaherty's purpose throughout the book. Moclair is indicted for his avarice and for endeavoring to make himself a king over the people. The priest continually preached to obtain more and more money and insisted that financial donations be a salient part of almost every holiday or special occasion. He made certain that the parochial residence was as costly and as grand as it could be and attempted to control all the activities the people were involved in. He even started a political association called the People's League, which he ruled dictatorially. Although he often talked of the English tyrants and the necessity for freedom, he was on close terms with the gentry and actually supported British rule and procedures.

But it was Moclair's obsession with money which first disillusioned Skerrett. Particularly at the time of the death of his young son did the schoolmaster notice the undue greediness of the priest. At the customary money offerings for prayers for the dead, the improper eagerness of Moclair was unduly evident. Skerrett reflected that the priest was more interested in the money offerings he would obtain than in assuaging the sorrow of the living.

Moclair's conduct during the wake and funeral also indicated another quality which Skerrett found especially reprehensible in a clergyman. So detached from and inured to misery and suffering do such as Moclair become that they seem to be machines rather than human beings. If, of course, they were properly living in an imitation of Christ's pattern, they would be deeply inbued with sympathy, compassion, generosity, and humanity. In Moclair's case, however, no touch of Christ exists. He is selfish and motivated only by what will increase his power and authority. He behaves like an unethical business man who can, nevertheless, hypocritically designate any action—no matter how unjust—as God's will.

In his depiction of Moclair, O'Flaherty has given one of the most thorough and convincing portraits of the jesuitical-type clergyman ever written. Father Moclair is etched in dark shades: he is hypocritical; he is treacherous; he can playact masterfully; he can use people one moment and then cast them aside the next; and he can be relentless in bringing vengeance and in carrying out personal vendettas. At one point, he gains Skerrett's support to help him in a campaign against one of the political rebels. As soon as Moclair has triumphed over the revolutionary, he then turns his full hatred against the schoolmaster. Especially reprehensible is Moclair's attitude toward Finnigan, the poteen smuggler. In his various public sermons Moclair denounced the use of this drink. He knew that Finnigan was selling this liquor illegally, but he refused to stop this situation because Finnigan was one of his most ardent supporters and always presented the priest with scandal, gossip, and secret information which Moclair found to be useful. Moclair's answer to a serious complaint about Finnigan's bootlegging is a statement to the effect that Finnigan is more or less to be excused because he knows no other trade. Yet in all other cases, Moclair persecutes with considerable success anyone he deems to be doing something improper. Usually he manages to drive his opponents or rivals out of Nara.

The influence of Moclair's activities on the hopes, fears, and peculiarities of a peasant community are masterfully indicated. In his various machinations, Moclair is not above making use of the peasants' superstitions if they will help him further his purposes. He performs religious services to remove alleged evil spirits when it is obvious that no such spirits are involved, and he can allow superstitions such as the rumor that "the curse of God" is upon Skerrett to persist. Willing to take any means to justify his purposes and goals, Moclair emerges as a sly and treacherous conniver—very believable, a creature of flesh and blood, and a worthy opponent who can defeat a spirit-exalting Skerrett.

The characterization of Skerrett, however, fails to achieve O'Flaherty's purpose. In the first place, much of the burden placed on Skerrett is due to his wife's becoming drunk and disorderly and, eventually, insane. Second, Skerrett is to blame for this development; he does not love his wife, and he is quick to seize upon every occasion to tell her so. Early in the novel he asserted that he was a fool to marry her, and he cursed their wedding day. He had married her only because she was pregnant by him, and he had hated her unattractiveness and dullness. When she became pregnant the second time, he never spoke kindly to her or showed her any affection, for the visual signs of her pregnancy increased his dislike; this distaste and hatred is labeled at one point by the author as "inhuman." When, however, his son was born (the first pregnancy of his wife had resulted in a miscarriage), he, for the first time, shows his wife some affection, which astounds and pleases her. But this affection is sporadic and disappears when their son dies in an accident. The only thing that could have held husband and wife together was seized by death.

As a result of her husband's antagonism and her sorrow over the death of the child, Kate Skerrett shuns her husband. She suffers several hysterical fits and behaves bizarrely. From this point she descends to drunkenness and torments Skerrett at every opportunity. She becomes a weapon for Moclair in his conflict with Skerrett and also causes the schoolmaster to lose prestige and respect among the islanders. Her insanity further adds to his difficulties. Yet instead of arousing sympathy for Skerrett, his wife's behavior appears to be almost fit retribution for his behavior toward her. Although he did not love her, it is possible that, if he had given her a bit of kindness and understanding in the first two years of his marriage, the ensuing turmoil would not have occurred. Rather than bringing out "the nobility of Skerrett's nature," Skerrett's relations with his wife have just the opposite effect.

Skerrett's character defects, which clash with O'Flaherty's narrative intentions, are also indicated in other relationships. Until he becomes an enthusiastic supporter of the Gaelic-language revival movement and the common people, Skerrett has been "pompous and arrogant"; he has usually ignored the people's greetings; he has also often been brutal, has picked fights at the slightest provocation, and has been filled with pride and callousness. In his own way, as Dr. Melia, the local physician, observes, he, like Father Moclair, "wants to be King of the island." In the second half of the novel Skerrett gradually becomes more human in dealing with the people. He shares a larger percentage of his fishing earnings with the islanders. He makes every attempt to draw closer to the populace by interesting himself in both farming and fishing problems and management. Yet his general attitudes come to irritate the people especially when he begins to stress doctrines they were generally not prepared for: "The new gospel of love for their language and traditional mode of living, together with a longing for national freedom, which he preached to them, made no appeal to these peasants who, like all peasants, were only too eager to sell any birthright for a mess of pottage. And Father Moclair, the man of progress and materialist, had the pottage."[49]

Through the influence of Dr. Melia, Skerrett begins to preach a form of philosophic anarchism which derived from Kropotkin. Skerrett comes to believe that money and its demands and concomitant aspects make love impossible. He urges the people to share their produce communally and to eschew purchasing such commodities as tea, drink, and tobacco. Skerrett argues that the people are simply bondslaves to the storekeeper. He maintains that they can survive by their earnings from the land and the sea alone. Yet this line of reasoning does little except arouse antagonism: "Although he proved to them again and again that they were being exploited evilly by the shop-keepers, they persisted in their mode of living. Even though they admitted that they were just as enslaved by the new-born gombeen-man class, 'of their own flesh and blood,' as they had been by the landowners, they went their way and shrugged their shoulders. People do not go back to primitive communism merely because it is proved to them that progress towards capitalist civilisation is slavery."[50]

Another aspect of Skerrett's personality which works to denigrate the notion of the schoolmaster's nobility is a lack on his part of intelligence, of tact, and of common sense. O'Flaherty at one point makes this comment about his protagonist: "Being essentially a rather stupid man, of very slow understanding, it was vitally necessary for Skerrett to rely on somebody of greater intelligence for a plan of life."[51] So foolish and arrogant is Skerrett that he rejects vitally needed assistance. When Harkin attempts to help, he is treated harshly by the schoolmaster, who does not, at this point in the novel, even wish to favor his friends with civility.

Instead of being sensible enough to support the faction opposed to Moclair, Skerrett denounces both groups and behaves in a way which alienates the few friends that he still has. At a crucial moment he rejects the aid of the rebel Ferris, who has always attempted to assist and support him. When young Crogan, risking a boycott that could affect his livelihood, helps Skerrett move his belongings and furnishings from his home secretly at night, Skerrett is not above screaming his denunciations to the skies and, hence, risking serious injury to a friend and good samaritan. When Skerrett is given refuge in an isolated hamlet on the island, the people risk religious excommunication and economic boycott in order to harbor the schoolmaster. Yet he turns on his benefactors and calls them cowards and damns them to hell. Skerrett's behavior may in this situation receive some extenuation because he is obviously very close to the oncoming insanity which shortly seizes him.

As he is presented in this novel, Skerrett could hardly be a hero, at least not in the ordinary sense of the term. Sean O'Faolain, however, who overstates the notion that Skerrett wins audience sympathy, explains Skerrett's character thus:

At first Skerrett seems a monster. Gradually the disasters which fall on the man enlarge his character, and win our complete sympathy so that he ends as a hero who began as a villain. He stands up against the police, the school Inspector, the gombeen man, every official of alien rule, the timid half-superstitious islanders, and his great enemy the Parish Priest, never with any worldly sense but always at least with the primitive honesty of his own natural instincts. . . . Out of it all comes a sense of terrifying wonder at the inexplicable cruelty of life, and of admiration for the heroic folly of every man who tries to meet it four square, and we do, finally, believe the closing judgment on Skerrett. "The nobility of his nature lay in his pursuit of godliness." . . . I need hardly say that O'Flaherty's image of godliness in not that of a professor of metaphysics.[52]

O'Faolain's interpretation of the novel is the way O'Flaherty himself means it to be understood; yet the last statement by O'Faolain concerning O'Flaherty's notion of godliness touches the heart of the matter.

Only if O'Flaherty's notion of godliness is accepted can the novel be adequately explained. The O'Flaherty hero here is again a Gargantuan figure: he is exaggerated and blown up beyond life. He is something of Byron, something of Nietzsche, something of Genghis Khan, something of Milton's Satan. He is supplied with far reaching hopes, ambitions, and lusts, and he frequently feels at one with nature and the wild, desolate aspects of the island which draws him "towards its savage bosom." His anger and sensuality continually blaze out against his ill fate. He is, by O'Flaherty's admission, "a wild, brutal man"; but he fulfills the notion of O'Flaherty's credo: "But what is beautiful in man is that he is unhappy as a man and wishes to be a god, to be free from death and the restraint of the earth's balance; that he wants to fly into space and loot the universe; that he is always hankering after the tree of knowledge; that he creates gods only in order to break them; that he is a being constantly in revolt and in his highest form, finding beauty only in wild tragedy."[53]

There are, however, too many loopholes to make the schoolmaster an appealing figure and to render the novel satisfactory. The black aspects of Skerrett's nature and his wild brutality outweigh or obliterate features which would have given him a humanity and a generosity that could arouse the reader's sympathy. Even if O'Flaherty's version of godliness is accepted, Skerrett does not have the intelligence or heroic stature to inspire the reader's admiration. Even when his schoolteaching descends to the level of eccentric incompetence, he presents a most impassioned defense of being a free and independent spirit.

In the light of Skerrett's deficiencies and inadequacies, the rhetoric, despite a mellifluous ring, suggests a lame and hollow rationalization of failure and foolishness rather than a justifiable apologia: "I'm sowing the seeds for the growing of a free race. That's what I'm doing. And these seeds'll grow in spite of you or Moclair, in spite of the whole gang of you. I'm a man, free and unsubdued. And when I die, if it be tomorrow, stoned to death by my enemies, I'll be remembered as a free man who never surrendered his faith or his independence. I'll stand out in the memory of the people as a man to be imitated, when skunks like you and Moclair are forgotten." [54]

Skerrett, unless he is accepted as an abstract Romantic principle, is definitely not to be imitated. Skerrett's version of "Arise, awake, or be forever fallen" clashes too contradictorily with O'Flaherty's over-emphasis of the schoolmaster's deficiencies and inadequacies. In Skerrett, the reader does not observe a human being; he sees a symbol, and this symbol and abstraction do not blend harmoniously with the literal and realistic context of the book.

If O'Flaherty had rendered Skerrett less a Romantic abstraction and less eccentric and bizarre in behavior and manner, the author would still have had to overcome several weaknesses apparent in the organization and development of the novel. O'Flaherty is still addicted to the habit of springing surprising and usually improbable changes and events upon the reader. Moreover, he does not give enough attention to the principle of narrative foreshadowing. Thus, at one moment we are informed that Dr. Melia, who admires the solitary type of life, plans to become a hermit; two pages later the doctor has fallen in love and has eloped to the United States. The change of fortune in the wealthy Athy family is also presented without logical preparation. Athy, the local squire, who represents hostile alien power and who seems to be in a solid and commanding position of influence when he first appears, suddenly falls into bankruptcy and is forced to bed with delirium tremens.

Other characters such as Ferris and Coleman O'Rourke, who seem at the beginning of the book to be significant figures, disappear for pages at a time and then are suddenly reintroduced as if the reader had just encountered them a few moments before. Indeed, the switch in Coleman O'Rourke's behavior defies belief. He is first presented as a rebel interested in the freedom and welfare of the people. As a consequence he tangles with Father Moclair, and at one point he has to be restrained from striking the priest. Eventually, Moclair manages to have O'Rourke arrested and imprisoned for a time. Later the fire-eating rebel O'Rourke becomes friendly with Moclair in one descriptive sentence: "O'Rourke was brought over by the reception through Moclair's influence of a fresh supply of trawling nets from the government authorities." [55] Later O'Rourke becomes perhaps Moclair's most aggressive and outspoken supporter. Such extreme switches of behavior might have been made credible if the novelist had taken more care and patience.

The possible effectiveness of this novel is decreased by the mere telling of many changes and the occurrence of new developments. The story's probability and verisimilitude would have been improved immeasurably if some of these startling changes and momentous occurrences had been shown as actually in the process of happening rather than being related in a few sentences. Too often in *Skerrett,* O'Flaherty seems to shrink from facing some of the most significant dramatic scenes; and this tendency also reduces the power of the book.

Another structural weakness is the final chapter, which is only a half-page in length. In this chapter O'Flaherty states the effect of Skerrett's and Moclair's posthumous reputations, and in these few lines we are told about Skerrett's nobility of nature and his "pursuit of godliness." But, after witnessing all the frailties and the brutality of Skerrett's nature, this last chapter and its comment seem, as we have already noted, anticlimactic and misleading.

Although O'Flaherty fails in his basic goal, he is extremely effective in demonstrating the essential fickleness and instability of the people. While he does not make Coleman O'Rourke's fickleness logical, O'Flaherty does manage to be persuasive in dealing with the farmers and fishermen as groups. These folk are swayed easily by clerical influence, economic advantages, superstitions, primitive notions, and the momentary power of an individual speaker also plays a part. For example, when part of Moclair's house is bombed, the people are so moved to sympathy that they turn the wily cleric into a martyr.

When Skerrett's earlier distaste for the people has been turned into enthusiasm for them, he and Dr. Melia engage in a debate. Melia, who does not believe in the integrity of the common man, asserts:

The mob loves only scoundrels. Being base itself, the mob only loves what is base. Being slaves they only love those who ill-treat and rob them. Look at Moclair. Look at Finnigan. . . . You are queer in their eyes, so even though you work for them they scoff at you and think you a fool, because you are not hoarding money and trying to persecute your neighbors. They'll stone you out of the island because of your honesty. I've come to the conclusion that, wherever there is a priest, a policeman and a shopkeeper, there can be no justice and no peace.[56]

Skerrett, at this point in the story, rejects Dr. Melia's pessimistic viewpoint and maintains that the people as a majority are right and sensible; they are simply misled by evil authorities such as Moclair. The physician responds that leaders such as Moclair are like the people, only much cleverer: "That's all. So he lives on them." Dr. Melia cautions Skerrett to leave the people alone; no good, he observes, can come from helping them. Although Skerrett attempts to reject this theory, the novel forcefully bears out the fact that Melia is correct. Skerrett, completely disillusioned, finally rages: "I've been a damn fool, trying to win the people's respect by becoming like themselves. They only respect the man that walks on them and despises them." [57]

If O'Flaherty had only humanized his schoolmaster protagonist to a more normal, likeable degree and made the teacher's conflicting characteristics credible, he could perhaps have illustrated his theme with persuasiveness. As it is, the sympathy aroused for Skerrett is too little and too sporadic to make the thesis successful. The evil of human nature and of such authorities as Moclair stands out powerfully and convincingly, but the character of Skerrett is too bizarre, too extreme, too much an iconoclastic Romantic projection to reach deeply into the mind and heart of the reader. Unfortunately, we cannot be sufficiently engaged with him to eliminate the feeling that he more or less deserves much of the trouble that falls upon him.

## V   The Martyr

While *The Martyr* is the last of what should be called the "melodrama of the soul" novels, it differs from the typical O'Flaherty narrative in that it focuses on four significant characters rather than on one figure and forms itself into a series of character portraits. Brian Crosbie, Jack Tracy, Major Joe Tyson, and Colonel Patrick Hunt, caught in the turmoil of the Irish Civil War, exemplify four different approaches to the problems of these troubled years.

When a group of rebels led by Crosbie and Tracy hold Sallytown in County Kerry, Crosbie's thoughts gravitate more and more to pacifism and religious purification; but Tracy and Angela Fitzgibbon, a fiery aristocratic woman rebel, urge more daring and aggressive military action. As the Free State government forces, under the direction of Hunt and Tyson, advance through the countryside, they eventually overwhelm the rebel stronghold at Sallytown. Crosbie and Angela Fitzgibbon are taken prisoner, while Tracy, wounded during the skirmish, and a few followers escape to a remote rural retreat. While the Free State troops continue to conquer and occupy more and more territory, Tyson determines to discredit Crosbie and deal a blow to the Republican cause. Tyson threatens that Crosbie will be killed unless he confesses his treason and calls upon all the remaining rebels to lay down their arms. If Crosbie refuses, Tyson promises him a horrible but secret death so that Crosbie cannot become a martyr symbol for the rebel bands. Since Crosbie will not repudiate the insurgent ideals, Tyson carries out the promised execution in a savage manner.

The central focus is on Crosbie who is widely known throughout the country. During the earlier rebellion against the British at the time of the Troubles, Crosbie wins attention and praise when he—as well as several others—participates in a hunger strike in order to call attention to English injustice and to bring about independence. But, although he is willing to endure suffering in order to eliminate British control, the idealistic Crosbie is reluctant to kill fellow Irishmen in the Civil War now taking place. He is, however, obsessed with making gestures of "protest against the national betrayal" and wishes to purify the national soul. In order to accomplish this goal, he insists that he and his followers keep their spirituality uncontaminated. He asserts that the spirit can be purified by martyrdom and not by shedding the blood of fellow countrymen who are enemies of the Republicans.

Crosbie is a mystic and a dreamer in a period when brother is pitted against brother in a country violently lacerated by all the particular cruelty and bitterness reserved to a Civil War. While taking part in a thirty-two-day hunger strike, Crosbie becomes more and more removed from his fellow men. He begins to thrive on solitude and meditation. He seeks God; and, when he looks upon the beauties of nature which manifest the Almighty, he feels even more isolated from his fellow revolutionaries. He now believes war is "immoral and useless," yet he has been enmeshed in the freedom struggle and forced into a position which he strangely appears not to have foreseen. His lack of foresight in this matter is further proof of his dreamy, impractical nature.

Crosbie decides that he personally can no longer fight. He had joined the Republican army because the adulation he received when he was on the hunger strike had tickled his vanity for a time, and he had thought it might be pleasant to continue as a hero amid the applause of the crowd. He also realized the difficulty of self-denial and the lonely hermitic life, so he believed mob security would be more rewarding.

But he has discovered that he cannot change his essential nature. He stresses that all individuals have different talents, and each man must pursue the particular endeavor marked out for him by his inclinations and by his destiny. Accordingly, Crosbie determines to choose a life that will be just the reverse of the existence of the typical members of both warring factions: "Prayer and contemplation and suffering are what appear to me most capable of purifying the souls of our people, and of making our country free and noble. So I'm leaving the fighting to those that have the stomach for it. I'm going to give up everything and become a hermit, to try and gain from God by self-denial and by prayer what I don't believe we can gain by fighting." [58]

Since Crosbie refuses to fight and kill, Tracy, his second in command, and his fellow Republicans believe that Crosbie is a coward. They are astounded when he tells them he is not going to flee from Sallytown since in their minds refusal to fight and the act of desertion are synonymous. Practicing his new philosophy, Crosbie deliberately allows himself to be delivered into the hands of the enemy; and he rationalizes his behavior as an act that will be acceptable to Christ. When Angela Fitzgibbon (a freedom fighter obviously patterned after real-life Constance Markievicz) attempts to stir Crosbie into action, he accuses her of being a murderess because she enjoys seeing men die. To counteraccusations that he has become insane, he responds: "This gibe of insanity is always hurled at any believer that lays bare his soul and rises above the dross of this world to the ecstasy of Divine contemplation." [59]

When Crosbie is captured by the Irish Free State forces, a struggle between Crosbie and Major Tyson of the Free Staters begins in earnest. Tyson surmises that Crosbie wants to be a marytr so that his death will be a living symbol to his countrymen of the need for freedom; consequently, Crosbie is intending to accomplish in death more than he could in life. Tyson loathes Crosbie, primarily because he abominates the religious views of his prisoner. Tyson, who is without a conscience, abhors the notion of prayer, suffering, and martyrdom; he insists upon direct, violent action. He believes that Ireland will grow under the Free State government and eventually completely control its own destiny.

He denigrates religion, claiming that Crosbie wants to make the country into a "prayer stool"; and, to him, Crosbie is a coward and has no real understanding of or respect for his viewpoint. Tyson's cruelty is widely known; and, when Crosbie cries out to Christ for religious assistance and for patience and perseverence to bear his suffering ("his cross"), the first inkling is given of what Tyson plans if Crosbie does not capitulate. Tyson threatens to help Crosbie "bear his cross" by giving him a cross and crucifying him.

Crosbie's request to see a priest raises a new issue. Deeply religious and sensitive, Crosbie typifies a noble form of spiritual feeling built on brotherly love and genuine idealism. Such a form of religion would seem to deserve wholehearted support from religious authorities, yet when Crosbie wishes to confess his sins so as to be prepared for execution by his Free State captors, the priest informs him that no member of the Irish Republican Army Irregulars can be given absolution. The bishops have excommunicated all Republican rebels until the insurgents acknowledge their errors and submit to the governmental authorities. The irony here is severe and telling; and, apart from the religious aspects of the question, the picture of the turmoil of a Civil War period is intensified. Although Crosbie is more truly spiritual than most of the members of the church, he is denied the religious consolation given by the formal religious organization of his country. Crosbie, like Joan of Arc, is a victim of the church as well as of the state.

Canon McElroy, who comes at Crosbie's request for the final religious rites, is willing to barter his privilege of bestowing absolution in exchange for Crosbie's word that he will give up his allegiance to the rebel cause. When Crosbie explains that he cannot violate his conscience, the priest denounces him since to the clergyman submission to religious authority is the most important factor involved. McElroy is so naive about political matters that he at first refuses to believe that Crosbie's life is to be taken by the government troops.

O'Flaherty again underscores another irony in the situation when the priest becomes violent about what he regards as Crosbie's recalcitrance and asserts that Crosbie should be flogged. On the other hand, Crosbie forgives the priest his lack of understanding and his refusal to grant absolution. Crosbie realizes that he is coming closer and closer to his martyrdom. His idealism, pure spirituality, and sense of Christly mission are foreign to the ideas of the priest.

When Crosbie refuses to recant and Tyson takes him alone on a car trip, the executioner still hopes that Crosbie will relent under the imminent threat of death and will, thereby, blacken the rebel cause. Tyson takes his prisoner to a remote rural location. He is the only one who knows Crosbie's whereabouts; and, if Crosbie does not return, Tyson alone will know the manner of his execution. When the two men arrive at the foot of a desolate mountain, Tyson fashions a rough wooden cross. He constantly reiterates that Crosbie can avoid such a death, but Crosbie clings to his principles. After being forced to carry the cross up the mountain, Crosbie is tied to the structure and the cross is set upright. Tyson executes his victim by setting fire to the cross and then weighting it so that it collapses and crashes down the side of the mountain. Crosbie receives his martyrdom, and his last words ask for God's mercy upon Tyson.

In the confrontation between executioneer and victim, their opposing views are incisively contrasted. Both men are doing what they regard as best for themselves and for their country. Both started with more or less the same ideals and goals; whereas Crosbie has turned to a religious response, Tyson, who has been bitterly disillusioned by religion in Ireland, hates Crosbie and what Crosbie represents because he himself formerly loved and believed deeply in religion and spiritual ideals. He presently believes that the state is supreme and is the only God, that nothing must interfere or stand in the way of state power, and that men must become machine-like and heartless for the good of the state.

Jack Tracy, who takes charge of Crosbie's Republican unit after the latter's desertion, operates with motives which differ from those of Crosbie and Tyson. The coarse, belligerent Tracy is fighting for the triumph of socialism. Like Tyson, he no longer believes in God or religion. He stands for social revolution and wants to have the working class control the country. Tracy supports the grand romantic gesture, and he dreams of a workers' utopia where justice will exist for all.

Another point of view current at the time is represented by Colonel Hunt, a pragmatist, who strives to clear up the disorder and entrench the power of the Free State government with the least amount of turmoil. Working for the consolidation of what will be the rule of the middle class, Hunt is all things to all men, now conciliating and compromising, now threatening, now cajoling, now cautious. His middle-of-the-road, bread-and-butter approach was historically to win out eventually as the most prominent strain in the Ireland of the 1930's and 1940's.

The divisions, madness, cruelties, confusion, and chaos of the period blur and intermingle with the variety of viewpoints, and O'Flaherty leaves an accurate impression of a savage and bizarre period when so many people were divided and fought for different reasons under different inspirations and did not really respect or understand one another's points of view. In the light of the many interesting characters and of the variety of attitudes found in the novel, *The Martyr* should have been a highly successful book; but again—as is true of so many O'Flaherty novels—the work blends much material that indicates considerable genius and much that is simply pedestrian.

Although Crosbie's unrealistic theories and viewpoints can be understood, he does not engage reader sympathy as he should. He is too often indecisive and seemingly unsteady in several of his motives and intentions. His pacifistic behavior is strikingly out of place in the Republican Army unit that he leads, and it strains the reader's credulity to believe that such a man—even remembering the patriotic support his hunger strike generated—could ever be chosen to direct a rebel fighting force. Crosbie's inactivity and obfuscation during the Free State attack on Sallytown make him appear even more spineless, and he tends to forfeit empathy in this regard alone. If this material had been deleted, Crosbie might not seem so confused and weak that his spiritual idealism is somewhat unconvincing. It is true that O'Flaherty also wishes to demonstrate the impracticalness and inappropriateness of Crosbie's sacrificial mysticism, but, as the novel turns out, Crosbie's mysticism is presented in such a farfetched and extreme manner that he appears, in general, too foolish, too unbelievable. We do not, therefore, receive a logical or balanced impression of one who belongs to what Yeats calls "the cult of sacrifice planted in the nation by the executions of 1916." As a consequence, O'Flaherty's attack on this sacrificial cult, which he regarded as too dreamy and too antithetical to badly needed social and political progress in Ireland, is not as effective as it could have been.[60]

Tyson's wish to crucify his prisoner is credible given Tyson's attitude toward religious ideas and his hatred of Crosbie, but the crucifixion itself is another matter. The carrying-out of this weird plan ends the novel with a scene that for sheer suspense and startling shock has few equals in modern fiction. The scene has been praised by William Faulkner, and Rebecca West declared it to be as "ghastly" and as "powerful" as one of Goya's "Désastres de la Guerra" series. Despite such praise, the ending is exceedingly farfetched and appears to have been included more for its sensationalism and shock value than as a credible narrative outcome of previous action. Here the melodrama becomes false and excessive.

The novel is also marred by character behavior which is improbable and not artistically prepared for. Canon McElroy is at first infuriated when he discovers that a political execution is about to take place in his parish. In his anger and in the midst of his protests he suddenly has a glass of liquor and becomes tranquil, forgetting his previous feelings about Crosbie. It is perfectly possible that McElroy could be swayed from his duty, but not so quickly and so baldly as O'Flaherty presents this happening. A gradual cooling of anger, some of Colonel Hunt's blandishments, and a few drinks could have been given in narrative depth; and, the Canon's sudden reversal of his position would not appear so artistically unwarranted.

The Free State Captain Sheehan's sudden shift from his position of loathing Tracy to an attitude very favorable toward the wild Socialist can also be cited as an example of questionable narrative manipulation. The change as it is presented is not sufficiently motivated and convincing. With patience and development, O'Flaherty could also have made this alteration of viewpoint credible; but, under the circumstances, he simply does not manage to do so.

Other narrative blunders appear. The story is described in such a way as to make everything work too patly against the rebels. In the various fighting engagements, they do absolutely nothing correctly. Their inaccuracy in shooting is utterly fantastic; their maneuvers are foolish and easily foiled; their soldiers—Rourke, for example—seem willing to confess quickly and give every bit of information possible. As a result of such pat techniques, the reader begins to doubt the occurrences and refuses to yield his "willing suspension of disbelief."

O'Flaherty has also unfortunately intruded a romance between Tracy and Kate McCarthy, which is very much out of place in the context. Love on a combat mission has a Hollywood ring, and it adds another element of skepticism about the authenticity of the story and detracts from the artistry which such a narrative should have.

Another weakness of the book is the traditional O'Flaherty reliance on very ordinary prose filled with clichés and flat word choice. He writes the first and easiest words which occur to him. It often appears that the author has not seriously given sufficient time or attention to what he is actually writing. For example, as Crosbie and Tyson climb the steep mountain to reach the place of execution, both men are wearied and exhausted from the effort. Yet the author now describes their behavior thus: "They hurried in silence across the level strip of thickly heathered ground." A few lines later, they are again collapsing and exhausted. The choice of the word "hurried" in this context is decidedly out of place and violates the whole spirit of this section. Words like "labored" or "struggled" would be much more logical and meaningful in this sentence. This example is not an isolated lapse, and such carelessness in diction detracts from the novel's effectiveness.

Despite these blemishes, *The Martyr* possesses significance because "individual passion is subordinated to the dialectic representation of several different attitudes,"[61] and the revolutionist type is examined with perception in four different possible guises: as mystic, as anarchist, as gunman, and as pragmatist. Tyson, Tracy, and Colonel Hunt, in particular, come alive and are vividly realized; and, while Crosbie is not persuasively described, his mysticism can be understood. Moreover, as O'Connor and other Irish writers have insisted, such mysticism plays an important part in the Irish spirit. The novel serves to emphasize that the people of Ireland combine "a capacity for mystic self-immolation, and at the same time, a ruthlessness" which Basil Davenport, for example, finds equaled only by the Russian temperament.[62]

*The Martyr* also contains several confrontations between characters, and it demonstrates anew O'Flaherty's gift for creating suspense in the genre of the psychological thriller. *The Martyr,* then, is a potpourri of splendors and miseries, of many effective qualities existing side-by-side with blunders which would not be tolerated in the work of a third-rate writer. Again, of course, the lack of discipline, the lack of the time and patience to work on and blend the materials to the highest artistry is evident. Sean O'Faolain's comments on *The Martyr* best epitomize a logical and balanced reaction to much of O'Flaherty's writing in the genre of the novel:

What an amazing writer O'Flaherty is! There is not another writer living who could have got away with *The Martyr*. It is full to the neck of faults and absurdities. . . . It is at times so crude as to be almost laughable, and so brutal as to be disgusting. Yet, when you put it down and think it over, every single one of the four main characters remains in the memory with just the same vital effect as life itself. Finally one puts away the book in a fury with the author for such extravagant waste of genius, for there is no use pretending that the novel satisfies. When one recovers from the bludgeon effect of his method one realizes that he could, if he would take pains, be one of the greatest writers living.[63]

CHAPTER 5

# *The Last Phase*

COMMENCING IN 1845, one of the most tragic disasters of
modern times occurred in Ireland. A blight descended on the
potato crop, the basic source of food for the country; and by
1851 the population had decreased by more than two and one-half
million. Death by hunger, fever, and concomitant disease killed over a
million and a half people; but nearly another million people managed to
board ships and flee to Canada, the United States, and other parts of
the world. The most ironic aspect of this situation was that Ireland
possessed, during this dreadful period of starvation and suffering,
enough corn and other food to feed its population; but this food was,
under governmental laws and procedures, exported to England. Few
events in modern history have exhibited greater governmental negli-
gence and misrule, and the reality of the misery of the people "in most
cases far exceeded description." [1] A topic such as the "Great Famine"
provided compelling material for a novelist. Yet no writer was able to
handle this heart-rending subject with the necessary artistic competence
and objectivity until O'Flaherty essayed the task; and his work, at
completion, became his most comprehensive and successful literary
achievement.

## I  Famine

This novel marked a distinct departure for O'Flaherty. Hitherto, he
had written about events which had occurred during his own lifetime,
particularly in the 1920's. Now as he turned to historical fiction, he
attempted to recapture a period which he knew chiefly from the
experiences of his ancestors and from history and tradition. Furthermore, he eschewed the "melodrama of the soul" or the ethical
detective-story approach and technique which had so pervaded his early
works of fiction. On account of the nature of the material and its

96

handling by O'Flaherty, *Famine* (1937) becomes just as important as a historical and social document presenting a problem of immense proportions as it does as a story or a study of human behavior.

The setting is County Galway—the mainland area near O'Flaherty's own native Aran Islands. The events, which commence in 1845, revolve about the family of farmer Brian Kilmartin. Kilmartin, seventy-one years of age, is Irish Gothic—steady and hard-working. His tenant farm under the ownership of an absentee landlord is not unduly prosperous, but the family by thrift and diligence is able to subsist adequately; and, although one of the sons calls it a life of "hunger and hardship," the Kilmartins are relatively fortunate in comparison to many of their neighbors. The children of the neighboring O'Hanlon family, for example, are frequently hungry because their father cannot find work.

The O'Hanlons, who are also carefully scrutinized by the novelist, have been continually aided by the generosity of the Kilmartins. The O'Hanlon family is typical of many squatters throughout Ireland who had been evicted from their former holdings. The land has constantly been sublet and divided into small holdings in order to obtain increased rent. The landlord or his agent can—and frequently did—force a tenant to leave his small parcel of land for any reason whatsoever. As a result of such tactics, the O'Hanlon children are emaciated because of having little to eat. They appear to be much older than their actual years, and they possess an air of perpetual despondency. They demonstrate that poverty and suffering dominate the countryside even in normal times. In addition to the typical problems of subsistence and survival, the Kilmartins have a tubercular son, twenty-four years of age. The effect of pinched economic circumstances and inadequate medical attention in this time and place is also underscored by the fact that tuberculosis has already brought death to five of the Kilmartin children.

While the Kilmartins, the O'Hanlons, and their neighbors pursue their traditional modes of subsistence, there comes news of a potato blight which is spreading throughout the country. This blight, which first appears in a nearby valley, shortly attacks the land of neighboring farmers, and the nauseating odor characteristic of the disease, commences to pervade the area. Although science now knows that the blight is caused by a fungus, "Phytophtora infestans," and multiplies rapidly under certain weather conditions, knowledge of the disease's cause was a mystery at the time of the Irish famine. When the rotting occurs the people are, therefore, bewildered and helpless. Even if the crop is dug prematurely and packed away in airtight trenches, the blight manages to reach some of the tubers. The Kilmartins are able to rescue only fifteen of the forty bushels which they had expected to harvest.

The ravages of the blight increase in a devastating fashion, but the agents of the landlords continue to demand rent charges in full. Even in ordinary times it becomes difficult for the tenant farmers to save money since it is usually owed to the landlord and the stores. When the potato crop fails, rent money is nonexistent. At this point early in the famine, the government still remains aloof. Rumors pass that the authorities will supply food. In addition, suggestions are heard that taxes will be lowered; and, with the residue money, provisions will be provided while work projects can supply additional money. Other proposals recommend that money be raised by taxing absentee landlords, that corn should not be exported but distributed to the people, and that grain should not be allowed to be used for distilling purposes.

As the situation worsens and as the people find it more difficult to pay rent, Chadwick, the landlord's agent for that Galway area, continues to demand full payment. Chadwick, who has absolutely no sense of understanding or humanity, is totally unconcerned about the potato blight or the possibility that the people face starvation. Avarice is his ruling passion; and, as long as he can collect rent, he is satisfied. For O'Flaherty, he symbolizes the general attitude of the gentry in Ireland and the controlling groups in both Erin and England. History testifies to the existence of such mercenary agents, but in the novel Chadwick seems to be unreal and artificial—a caricature, a stereotyped villain out of melodrama. His behavior is so irrational and his vices are so exaggerated—his desire to lash Mary Kilmartin, for example—that he jars the verisimilitude of the story. The characterization of Chadwick is one of the few aspects of *Famine* that is not handled with artistry.

When the people are forced to resist Chadwick's unreasonable demands, they are evicted or their animals are seized in lieu of rent payment. Since the potato crop of 1845 has failed and since the only remaining commodity the people possess consists of their cows and other livestock, they now have little chance to survive. Even the Kilmartins are deprived of their livestock because they are unable to meet the rent payment for the first time owing to the famine and to the expenses attending the death of their consumptive son. They are left with only a newly born calf which must be immediately killed because its mother has just been taken away by Chadwick's myrmidons, and no means exist to feed the animal and keep it alive. Ironically, the activities of the land agent are fully supported by the law courts.

Without losing objectivity in portraying the events taking place, O'Flaherty indicates that a little mercy and a little common sense would have helped alleviate much of the people's misery at this particular time. One of the tenants, who has become insane because of the general misery and is sent to the madhouse, is relatively fortunate; he at least receives a quart of milk and two pounds of bread daily, whereas the average farmer has almost little or nothing to eat.

Hope returns the following year when the potato crop appears to be heavy and successful, but again the blight comes in July and conditions become incredibly horrid. "Famine fever" and typhoid cause additional deaths;[2] one mother commits euthanasia because she cannot bear to see her starving children suffer any longer; there are mass burials in large common graves; starved dogs rend an aged man; the workhouse is so jammed that people wait outside daily in the hope that some inmates will die so that their places may be taken. But, in the midst of the most intense period of deprivation and misery, the people watch as grain and oats, guarded by soldiers, are taken out of the country and sent to England. The scenes reflect a living chamber of horrors comparable in many ways to such occurrences as the Black Plague and Hitler's pogroms—periods when justice and human decency seem to have vanished from the world. O'Flaherty describes the situation with a completely detailed obsession with the misery and desperation.

To the credit of his art, O'Flaherty's narrative approach—direct, documentary, matter-of-fact—manages to convey the degradation and horror without either sentimentality or a note of falseness. Such a subject as the famine could easily be melodramatically overpainted and lack authenticity. O'Flaherty attempts to retain a basic impassiveness and objectivity about the scene and situation he is describing by pretending to be a storyteller who knows the events from oral tradition, family records, and historical documents. His use of phrases such as "Nowadays it is hard to imagine the degree of snobbery prevalent in those days," "As we shall see," "I am certain that," and "I must remark at this point" gives the narrative a personal aspect without involving the author so deeply in the story that the necessary objectivity is dissipated. This approach also adds a reasoned, researched, carefully thought-out quality which makes the relation more factual. This technique is blended with a Naturalistic accumulation of documentary detail; for example, local newspapers and a letter to America are quoted, and constabulary regulations are given (the police were "to hang about ditches, plantations, and above all to make domiciliary visits, always taking their telescopes with them on day patrol and rockets at night").[3] Some of the quotations used by O'Flaherty are obviously fabricated; others are genuine. The total impact of such touches is compelling, and the verisimilitude is immeasurably increased.

In the light of O'Flaherty's other writings, his objectivity in this novel is unexpected and surprising. A subject such as the famine could arouse the average Irishman to anger and even maudlin brooding; but O'Flaherty, despite his intensely emotional nature, attempts to present a wide variety of viewpoints about almost every aspect of the situation. He presents the attitudes of the authorities as well as the thoughts of the natives, and the people themselves are shown to possess several shortcomings. For instance, the misery caused by the potato blight could be alleviated to at least some degree by the people themselves if they could shift from a one-crop frame of mind and plant such vegetables as cabbages and, in general, attempt to vary their crops. But they are so tradition-bound that they refuse to alter their customary practices and habits. Or they could cooperate with Mr. Coburn, the Protestant minister, a kindly, well-disposed clergyman who makes several sincere efforts to help them; but their suspicions are too intense. Protestants are regarded as mean and treacherous; and even Father Roche, who is described as being relatively charitable, is bigoted and unthinking enough to believe that Coburn only wishes to help in order to make Protestant converts.

The matter of Coburn presents a serious indictment of the narrow attitudes of the people. Coburn gives the people any money he can spare, tries to have the government officials adopt humane measures, and asks for mercy and generosity on the part of the land agent. In brief, Coburn attempts to be a practicing Christian in every sense of the word. Yet the farmers, in their superstition and bigotry, destroy his garden and wreck his relief headquarters. Thus the tendencies to religious suspicion and general division once more work against the welfare of both the country and its people. Coburn is misunderstood and reviled because of past events and because of the present refusal to accept men of goodwill no matter what their persuasion.

Although his personal attitude is known, O'Flaherty even holds his temper when he treats of the village grocers and businessmen ("gombeen men") who seek to enrich themselves at the expense of the people.[4] Such is storekeeper John Hynes. Hynes arranges to purchase cheap Indian corn imported from the United States and profiteer by controlling its price. Instead of the government's distributing this corn at cost price, Hynes and men of his kind manage to offer and sell this commodity at a profit. Even Hynes's own son admits that he would allow the people of the community to starve rather than distribute the yellow meal on credit. Yet Hynes continues to believe that he is behaving sensibly in the interest of good business, and he even convinces himself that God is on his side. Again history bears out the truth of O'Flaherty's characterization.

Peculiarly enough, the policies of the government enable unscrupulous businessmen like Hynes to thrive. Although food depots exist, the government will not make these goods available to the people if the storekeepers have food to sell. The authorities insist that giving the people free food while the storekeepers exist to sell it would injure legitimate business. Since wealthy "gombeen men" like Hynes can always purchase food, the food depots remain closed; and more and more people starve.

In only one area of the novel does O'Flaherty really slacken the tight rein he holds on the story's objectivity. Surprisingly enough, knowing O'Flaherty's consistently anticlerical views, Father Roche utters a passage that is more characteristic of O'Flaherty's own personal feelings than those of a clergyman of this era:

Now he realised, as he walked, that it was the policy of "peace at any price," preached by him and by all the other priests and politicians in command of the great Repeal Association, that had produced this catastrophe, a disillusioned, disheartened, disorganized people at the mercy of the tyrannical government. A few short months ago, less than a year ago, if the bugles of war had been sounded, a million men would have been ready, armed with the frenzy of revolutionary faith, to crush the feudal robbers that oppressed them. But the demagogue O'Connell had professed himself a pacifist and a loyal subject of Her Majesty. The bishops also preached peace and obedience to the laws that gave them fat bellies and rich vestments and palaces. All those in command said that life must be spared and that no cause was worth the shedding of a single man's blood. Now that blood was going to rot in starved bodies; bodies that would pay for the sin of craven pacifism the punishment that has always been enforced by history.[5]

O'Flaherty becomes so emotionally involved at this point that he violates the logic of the narrative and his characterization of the priest. Father Roche, a conservative, is deeply committed to the righteousness of what he conceives to be the church's position, and he would not have thought of the "fat bellies and rich vestments and palaces" phrases because he would simply not acknowledge that such ideas have validity. O'Flaherty would not have been guilty of this artistic flaw if he had given these sentiments to the liberal and rebel-oriented curate, Father

Geelan; but to give them to the diehard Father Roche mars the objectivity and admits material completely inappropriate to a character's viewpoints.

This same anger of the author against the clergy for not activating movements against British control is underscored later in the novel when John Hynes's son realizes that Father Geelan, the prorevolutionary curate, was "a voice crying alone in the wilderness; a revolutionary soldier disarmed by the soutane which he wore and by the mitred felons to whom he had vowed obedience."[6] It is part and parcel of O'Flaherty's antagonism toward the clergy that the priests did not assist in the struggle for Irish independence; indeed, they thwarted it at almost every opportunity. O'Flaherty's quarrel with the church finds subjective expression in the two cited passages. But, as the Belfast historian R. M. Henry points out, the church in Ireland "has always been on the side of law and order. It has had a strong bias towards constituted authority, as was to be expected from a branch of the most conservative institution in the world. It excommunicated the Fenians, it opposed the Land League, it condemned the Rising. It is hardly too much to say that Ireland would have been ungovernable but for the influence of the Church."[7]

Throughout the novel O'Flaherty stresses the value of a united rebellion against British rule. Approval is implied for "the people against the tyrants" and "We'll crush the tyrants that suck our blood" sentiments whenever they are uttered by characters. An aura of blessed halo-like approval is placed around Thomsy Hynes's talk and his dream about the Young Irelanders' movement, the rebel group which manages to smuggle Kilmartin's son and daughter-in-law safely out of the country. Father Geelan, whose views obviously support O'Flaherty's position, declares that, if the church cannot obtain liberty for the people, then it should support rebellion and the sword, which will eventually win justice. Father Geelan's own character is presented as faulty because, although he utters noble sentiments for freedom and justice, he is too closely bound to the church's rules to violate its authority. As soon as Father Roche threatens to have Geelan unfrocked, Geelan reluctantly bows to his superiors and to the church. O'Flaherty does not condemn Geelan for this behavior, but the implication is clear. Enlightened and freedom-loving clergymen exist in Ireland, but they are held in bondage by the authority of the church. From time to time, the church's reluctance to support rebellion against British rule is indicated, but only in the "fat bellies" and "mitred felons" passages does O'Flaherty really lose his objective control to a reprehensible degree.

Just as on the two occasions quoted do O'Flaherty's own feelings—although his general attitude can be deduced—seem to get the better of his stern control, it is observable that O'Flaherty possesses a deep sympathy and compassion for the poor. Their plight is touching to both the author and the reader, although the author endeavors to remain objectively apart from their problems. In these circumstances, O'Flaherty tends to forget his relatively aloof pose when he commences Chapter XLIII with the following narrator's comment:

When government is an expression of the people's will, a menace to any section of the community rouses the authorities to protective action. Under a tyranny, the only active forces of government are those of coercion. Unless the interests of the ruling class are threatened, authority remains indifferent. We have seen how the feudal government acted with brutal force when the interests of the landowner were threatened, even to the extent of plundering the poor people's property. Now it remains to be seen what that same government did when those poor lost . . . the potato crop which they had sown.[8]

This statement is as close as O'Flaherty comes at any point in the novel to intruding his own attitudes about the government's treatment of the poverty-striken—except, of course, in his handling of characters such as Father Roche.

O'Flaherty retains a remarkably well-balanced presentation of the people's general probing of the disaster. In general, the bewildered people are dumbly attempting to understand their continued destitution and misfortune. Some claim there is a curse on the land, others insist there is a curse on the people. Most regard the situation as indicative of God's will, and they accordingly accept their deprivations. They offer prayers and say rosaries; they call upon God's mercy; they recommend trust in God and the acceptance of God's intentions, and they continue to proclaim that God is powerful and that God is good. Brian Kilmartin, for instance, can maintain that God has brought the famine in order to force people to think about their sins. When the people repent, then God and the earth will yield riches.

In recording such ideas and attitudes O'Flaherty is being faithful to Irish history. The people themselves were baffled by the actions of divine Providence, but most of them meekly accepted the situation as they experienced it and felt that in some way the inscrutable purposes of God's will were at work and that, in the long run, things would work out for the best.

There were, however, individuals such as Mary Kilmartin who espoused a more active philosophy. Mary, the most impressive figure in the book and one of the few sympathetic portraits of a woman in

O'Flaherty's fiction, argues that prayer is insufficient and that the people themselves are the salient factors in improvement of their plight. Her own example of hard work, steadiness, and determination is inspiring. Although depression and despair abound about her, she manages to bring a note of hope and perseverance to the situation. She even manages to arouse Brian, her father-in-law, to activity when for a time he despairs and loses the desire to persevere. Survival is more meaningful to her than the land or any aspect to be considered. Her youthfulness, the welfare of her infant, and her highly practical nature make her realize that the only worthwhile solution is escape to America. Mary, who decides she cannot perform her religious duties, rebels against divine Providence since God is certainly not doing anything to help the starving poor and seems to favor the wealthy.

Yet Mary's antireligious attitude is counterbalanced by the behavior and views of the second most admirable character in the novel, Brian Kilmartin. Aged, grizzled, and rock-hewn, he can be overly harsh and fierce, especially with his wife Maggie but never with his consumptive son Michael. The best food and loving kindness are always extended to his son, no matter how unbearably Michael behaves. The father continually gets up at all hours of the night to tend his son and to sit beside him as long as necessary. Kilmartin, while not excessively religious, accepts all as the will of God. He cannot pretend to understand the mysterious activities of the Divine Being, but he accepts the premise that such occurrences must ultimately redound to the betterment of man—if not in this existence, then in some other form of life.

Kilmartin also has a passionate devotion for the land, and no more dedicated farmer exists in the area. His ability to tend animals is legendary, and his patience in such matters is unending. Although he must take one blow after another—the loss of livestock, the death of his consumptive son, the destruction of his beloved crops, gnawing starvation—he towers over the scene of desolation. Except for a short while, Kilmartin, like his daughter-in-law Mary, continues to struggle and persevere, to do everything possible to help conquer tragedy. At the end of the book he must attempt to bury his wife Maggie with his own hands, but, so hungry and so emaciated that he cannot complete his task, collapses and dies on his beloved earth, meeting his dismal end with incredible courage. Even in death Kilmartin is an epic and enduring figure, all the more compelling because he has been drawn objectively with weaknesses and strengths; yet in O'Flaherty's handling he is presented as an individual who, in the most demoralizing circumstances possible, is a credit to humanity.

In addition to Mary and Brian Kilmartin, one other character in the novel stands out as a particularly memorable figure: Brian's brother-in-law, Thomsy Hynes. Thomsy has signed over his share of his sister's land to the Kilmartins in exchange for room and board; as a result, he loses initiative and becomes a drunkard. A lovable and picturesque figure, he is amusing when he is forced to give up his tattered clothes and take a bath; he provides encouragement and optimism when the family badly needs a cheering note; he acts with bravery when Martin is wounded and is forced to become a fugitive; and he is capable of starving himself so that Mary and her infant will have a little more to eat. Thomsy is not only one of the best-rounded characters O'Flaherty has ever portrayed, but he demonstrates the rare quality that is almost nonexistent in O'Flaherty's works—he is lovable. He is drawn with a sense of humor, generosity, and mellowness, attitudes which would have rendered O'Flaherty's *dramatis personae* more humane and agreeable if he had chosen to draw on these resources more often.

The fact that only three characters are especially notable is explained by observing that the people in the story undergo, in John V. Kelleher's words, a diminution against the "endless background of death. . . . The people . . . at last become quiet and inarticulate as death comes near around them." There is no "purgation for the pity and terror O'Flaherty has so brilliantly aroused."[9] Professor Kelleher argues that the novel possesses a defect because of the nature of the situation in which the characters are caught. This observation is unquestionably true, and yet this fault is attributable to this historical event itself rather than to the author or to his handling of the material.

Another feature is the comprehensiveness, or what one reviewer calls the "exhaustive detail,"[10] of O'Flaherty's historical commentary. He presents every phase of the disaster from the Quakers' well-intentioned but futile attempts to relieve hunger to the public-works projects which are eventually adopted. O'Flaherty's analysis of these projects is acutely accurate and sharply ironic. These relief works were supported on money loaned to Ireland by the British government. The Irish were charged five percent interest on these loans, but very little useful work could be undertaken since reclamation and the establishment of industries were forbidden. Road-building and land clearance were conducted but in a most inefficient manner; the workers were paid little; and only a small fraction of the total number of applicants could secure jobs. In the Black Valley district only three hundred of the one thousand needy applicants obtained work. Through mismanagement, wages were delayed, and the workers grew even weaker with hunger.

The officials who ran these projects were imported from England,

and they were more interested in increasing their own incomes rather than in helping the Irish. Bureaucracy increased; waste and futility were rampant. After a few months, the British authorities decided to stop the projects. O'Flaherty particularized this situation by having Patsy O'Hanlon work on a typical project from its commencement to its conclusion, and the characteristics and follies of this endeavor are visualized.

Equally striking as the novel's comprehensiveness is the vivid total impression left with the reader. O'Flaherty not only presents a historically accurate picture of the most dismal event in Irish history, he also brings authentic people to life—authentic people who undergo this terrible experience—while the causes and effects of the experience are analyzed and presented in depth. *Famine* must be linked with such famous novels as Emile Zola's *La Terre* and John Steinbeck's *The Grapes of Wrath* as books more or less in the Naturalistic tradition which uncompromisingly and vividly probe the sights of suffering and deprivation of farming folk with somber thoroughness. *Famine* is an unforgettable book because its scenes of misery and despair sear the memory; and this quality, as well as the nature of the tragedy, gives the book an epic grandeur.

Sean O'Faolain describes *Famine* as an "almost Biblical" novel: "The Irish *Exodus* in which there is no Moses to lead out the people of Israel."[11] Horace Reynolds has given the best description of the book's total impact and its position in the canon of O'Flaherty's works: "This novel marks an advance in seriousness and restraint if not in flash and brilliance. If it lacks the drive and excitement of his studies of men mad with some conflict of soul with circumstance, it is a richer, deeper novel. . . . Over all is an informing pity and compassion for the people, his people, whose tragedy he has written. The result is a convincing historical novel. Finishing it we say, certainly this is the way it must have been."[12]

## II.   *O'Flaherty's Most Recent Novels*

After reaching his artistic zenith with *Famine*, O'Flaherty projected second and third volumes of a historical trilogy about significant periods of Irish history.[13] *Land*, the second book in the trilogy, appeared in 1946, nine years after *Famine; Insurrection*, the final volume, was issued in 1950. Since the not-much-more-than-competent quality of these novels indicates that the long amount of time which passed before they appeared did not help to improve the author's work, it is evident that O'Flaherty had little left to say and that his natural indolence now began to dominate his career. Over a period of thirty years, from 1938 to the present, O'Flaherty has written only two novels and a relatively small number of short stories.[14]

*Land*, which is set in County Mayo in the late 1870's and early 1880's, considers the period when the word "boycott" came into use as a device to force the English landowners and agents to deal more equitably with the native population of Ireland. The oppressions and evictions especially characteristic of this period and the accompanying reprisals by the Fenians and the Land Leaguers seem subjects for a turbulent, appealing book. To be sure, the material could not rival as a subject the somber terror and hopelessness of the famine; nevertheless, the tenants' revolt possessed enough ore for a subject of rich resources. The result in *Land* is, however, a most disappointing novel. It contains some effective episodes, and the character of the Byronic Raoul St. George exerts a fascination at times. But, in general, the book fails, a failure all the more conspicuous because of the potential of the subject.

What O'Flaherty has done is to stereotype his characters, making them puppets, and to write as if he were producing a script for a historical saga à la Hollywood. Captain Butcher, a powerful and brutal landlord, plays the role of a typical "heavy," and young Michael O'Dwyer, the brave and handsome freedom fighter, and Lettice, the daughter of Raoul St. George and the girl with whom O'Dwyer falls in love, furnish the romantic interest—an interest which is obviously superimposed and out of place in what should be a realistic context. O'Dwyer is eventually killed in the struggle against British oppression, but the narrative is allowed to end happily when O'Dwyer's child is born in an atmosphere of hope for the future. With the new generation comes the belief that men and events are marching inexorably to bring eventual freedom.

Another unsatisfactory phase of the book is the bald contrast between the "bad" priest—the authoritarian, jesuitical Father Costigan—and the "good" priest, Father Kelly, a Fenian barred from performing his priestly duties. Such a contrast is legitimate in itself and could have been handled with the credibility found in the Father Roche—Father Geelan episodes in *Famine*. But in *Land* O'Flaherty's treatment of the two priests so lacks subtlety and ingenuity that the effect becomes a humorous parody rather than what the author actually intended—a genuine indictment of clerical conservatism and dogmatism.

Although O'Flaherty has ruined the general credibility and genuineness of his narrative by a hackneyed plot and by characters geared primarily for a second-rate cinema story, he does manage several effective strokes. The pathos of tenant eviction is sharply delineated, and the contrast between an elegant garden party at the magnificent estate of the Mongooles and the misery of the tenants is realistically and acceptably conveyed.

O'Flaherty is also true to his material when he pictures the peasants in their various superstitions and weaknesses. Often exceedingly devious, unreliable, and too easily led by feelings and prejudices, the farmers promote much of their own misery by failing to work together, by a facile willingness to be misled by glib talkers, or by momentary signs of improvement. Although at times O'Flaherty seems to fall into the "noble peasant" trap, he is usually clear-headed enough to acknowledge that the character faults and weaknesses of the land dwellers are many and that they are in various ways blamable for their deplorable situation.

Furthermore, despite his failure to handle the Father Costigan–Father Kelly contrast with subtlety, O'Flaherty sets forth the role of the church in matters pertaining to British rule with much insight and truth. The church's attitude toward the Fenians and to land-reform agitation and its belated realization that some compromise has to be made with the Land League movement illustrate the church's tendency to adapt itself to changing circumstances. Sean O'Faolain's historical commentary on the church's chameleon-like moves in such matters is demonstrated most sharply in this novel.[15]

In addition to the positive achievements just mentioned, it is quite apparent that O'Flaherty has not lost his strong narrative drive: he continues to be a teller of tales, a yarn-spinner. No matter how hackneyed the basic Hollywood plot of *Land* becomes, it still carries the power to force the reader onward.[16] This ability is all the more surprising in *Land* because of the obvious Hollywood story line, the oversimplified division of "good" and "bad" characters, and the relation of necessary background information which is inserted without subtlety (it is either stated baldly in dialogue or else is injected in expository passages).

In short, although *Land* possesses some redeeming aspects, it represents a definite decline from O'Flaherty's much more deeply researched and much more genuinely true and authentic *Famine*.

The book is also handicapped by Victorian and old-fashioned clichés. For example, O'Flaherty can write "Lettice threw herself against his bosom and cried in rapture"; and he still tends to interject comments which seem more authorial than typical of the characters. He can, for instance, allow one of his characters to remark, "We have been living since then like people besieged by Red Indians, in one of Fenimore Cooper's frontier outposts."

*Insurrection*, the third book in the historical trilogy, turns to the Easter Rebellion of 1916 for its subject. Bartly Madden comes to Dublin after working in a factory in England. With his savings, Madden plans to return to rural Connemara and settle on a farm. Before he manages to leave Dublin, he is robbed and forced to wander around the city. Suddenly the seizure of the General Post Office takes place, and the Irish Volunteers and the Citizen Army take up arms against the British authorities and their supporters. Madden is befriended by a Mrs. Colgan, whose son is one of the rebels against British rule; and, primarily through her influence, he is persuaded to join the insurgents.

He serves in a unit of the Irish Volunteers captained by Michael Kinsella, a dedicated and talented military leader who intensifies Madden's patriotic convictions. In the group is George Stapleton, an idealistic poet, whose attitudes and courage surprise Madden. Madden, Kinsella, and Stapleton fight through several skirmishes; and, although outnumbered and lacking sufficient ammunition, they perform heroically and courageously. Eventually, the three give their lives for the cause of Irish independence.

This book, which O'Flaherty once told the O'Hehir family was his favorite,[17] is different from O'Flaherty's other novels in that it is almost sheer action and description of action. The reader is immediately carried into the turbulent crowds which move in constant tide about the Nelson Pillar in O'Connell Street, and he becomes caught up in a Republican parade which soon turns from a perfunctory gathering into a mass dynamic movement to seize the General Post Office. At this point, the vortex of action is unceasing. The sound of the rifle firing, the disorder of the crowds, the futile cavalry charge, the blazing buildings, the looting of stores, and the bizarre unreality of street warfare—all these features of the Rising are recorded with vividness and move the story quickly to a crescendo. Throughout the novel, O'Flaherty's emphasis is on externals, and the narrative generates both suspense and swift story movement.

But, while the book is well handled on the external level, it does not possess the penetrating analysis of characterization and the in-depth detail which the subject deserves. In presenting externals O'Flaherty has neglected to develop his characters and to give them the dimension of credible people. Bartly Madden, whose choice as protagonist indicates a return by O'Flaherty to the earlier primitive heroes like Gypo Nolan, has little of the flesh-and-blood quality of Gilhooley, Skerrett, or the other credible protagonists in O'Flaherty's fiction; O'Flaherty once said that Madden was modeled on Padraic Pearse, but the resemblance is most remote.[18] Madden never comes fully alive; he is never convincingly observed from the inside. Moreover, Madden's shifts of viewpoint in favor of the insurgents and Mrs. Colgan are too sudden and unstable; these alterations of his attitude are not adequately prepared for, nor are they fully developed with narrative logic. Madden is the typical O'Flaherty chameleon protagonist; but, unlike many of the earlier central figures in the novels, he is characterized by too many improbabilities both in thought and in action. Madden too often appears to have been given short shrift by his creator. He is too often merely externalized; and, when his ideas are conveyed, they are indicated in a very sketchy manner.

Another apparent aspect in the portrayal of Madden is that, although he is intended to undergo much of the torment and mental anguish found in the pivotal figures of the early novels, he simply does not possess the depth of emotion or feelings of intensity evident in earlier narratives. O'Flaherty has lost some of his fire and verve; he lacks the frenzy and fury of his earlier work. The "fiery ecstasy" has, to a considerable degree, burned out. As a result, Madden becomes a pale figure lacking the distinguishing stature of a truly tormented character.

Lacking the fury and intensity which might give him a special glow, Madden and his superhuman feats of bravery and strength become improbable and melodramatic. He does not seem to possess the stature to accomplish such deeds. One of the characters describes Madden as "a primeval creature, utterly remote from my consciousness and unpredictable"—the way O'Flaherty would like Madden to be taken by the reader. But, because of O'Flaherty's inept and careless handling, the reader's impressions of Madden are simply not such.

O'Flaherty's treatment of the other figures in the novel is also uninspired. One of the measures of his considerable failure in this regard occurs when he fumbles the opportunity of presenting a credible portrait of the poetic George Stapleton. The sensitive and esthetic Stapleton, who abhors bloodshed and whose poor health disqualifies him from regular military service, feels that it is his patriotic duty to fight for the freedom of his country. Stapleton, a pantheist who exalts the idea of love, believes that he has now reached "la hora de la verdad" and that in participating in the crusade for independence, he has reached the real purpose of his existence and demonstrates the essence of his nature.

Since Padraic Pearse and several of the other participants in the

Easter Rising are of a poetic cast of mind and spirit, the appropriateness of having a figure such as Stapleton play a prominent part in the story is more than justified. Stapleton as a character, however, never seems authentic. O'Flaherty has given him several melodic lines and some mystical sentiments to utter, yet Stapleton is not two-dimensional. An outline character, he has no depth of portraiture. Again, O'Flaherty's cursory and incomplete attempts at characterization must be criticized.

Defects of characterization also vitiate the character of Michael Kinsella. Kinsella is meant to be presented as a dynamic leader whose courage and strength can attract a man like Madden and cement him more firmly to the cause. Madden's refusal to believe that Kinsella is dead and his long period of mourning over the body of his dead leader appear as exaggerated and improbable aspects of behavior since Kinsella does not appear, from O'Flaherty's handling, to be capable of eliciting such reactions. Kinsella could have been drawn as a vibrant and accomplished master of leadership and daring; however, O'Flaherty again fails to develop successfully an important character. If O'Flaherty had been energetic and given the same attention to characterization and depth of situation evident in *Famine*, then this novel of the Rising might have reached truly significant proportions. As Walter Kerr once observed, *Insurrection* is only "a piece of a novel . . . oblique and fragmentary. There is a big book to be made out of the materials, a book which will organize and relate every side of the experience."[19] In short, O'Flaherty needed to handle *Insurrection* the way he had treated *Famine*.

*Insurrection*, then, is unrewarding in toto because of weak and unconvincing characterization. It does possess a quick-paced narrative drive and does give a marvelously vivid pictorial sense of the Rising. The book puts the reader into the midst of the rebellion, and while more stirring and appealing than *Land*, it lacks a necessary philosophic mood of analysis and point of view.

## III  *Recent Short Stories*

In addition to producing two novels in the 1940's and 1950's, O'Flaherty also wrote a number of short stories. One of the best of this group is the title story of the collection *Two Lovely Beasts and Other Stories* (published in America in 1950). "Two Lovely Beasts" focuses on the problem of the man who wishes to be superior to other farmers. Colm Derrane ponders and considers purchasing a second yearling even though no one in his area of the countryside has ever managed to rear two calves at the same time, since the soil is poor and each farm is small. The lure of possessing two lovely animals and his confidence in his own ability to do the exceptional deed exert a continual fascination and challenge, respectively. Since, according to the custom of the area, the farmer who possesses milk has to share it with those who do not, the purchasing of a second calf will mean that some milk which is supposed to be given to neighbors will now have to be used to nourish the young cow. Derrane's obsession, however, is such that he decides to purchase the animal.

He is ostracized by his neighbors when they discover that he has taken the second calf and has violated the unwritten law in this part of rural Ireland. Even the woman who has pestered him to buy the second calf becomes hostile and also regards him as an outcast and an enemy. But Derrane is impervious to their reactions; for he becomes more and more entranced with the growing beauty of his two calves and believes them capable of becoming champions, and he grows more ruthless toward even his own family. He is willing to decrease his family's food rations in order to give his animals as much milk as possible, as well as the best of the fish and other available food.

Derrane wishes to rise in the world, and he insists that his present course of behavior will lead to that result. Although his parsimony and stringent form of existence work much hardship on his family, he persists in his single-minded aim; and he is able in time to open a store, although he continues to find envy and hostility. Nevertheless, he drives himself forward in his purpose, a successful but ruthless man.

Two main themes are observable in this story. One concerns the irony of fate: if Kate Higgins's cow had not died while giving birth to a beautiful calf, Derrane would not have gotten the idea to purchase the calf and start his rise to wealth. Yet, while Derrane prospers, the loss of her cow and the financial problems arising therefrom eventually lead Kate Higgins to an asylum and bring death and extreme hardship to the members of her family. The rise of one family parallels, therefore, the decline of another.

Although O'Flaherty rarely intrudes authorial comment in his short stories, it is not difficult to know that he does not approve of Derrane's conduct. Derrane achieves success and wealth; but Andy Gorum, the patriarch of the village, makes a statement which appears akin to the writer's point of view: "Whoever tries to stand alone and work only for his own profit becomes an enemy of all."[20] Later in the narrative Gorum predicts that disaster will visit Derrane because he has attempted to "stand alone and rise above the people." Derrane has injured his fellow humans by rejecting communal and collectivist standards. Some of O'Flaherty's own Socialist sympathies are evident here.

In "The Touch," which contains another closely observed and recorded segment of Irish country existence, a young rural worker who loves the farmer's daughter is discouraged because he is penniless and the farmer will not give approval for the marriage. Although the girl is willing to defy her father's wishes because of her love for the young man, he lacks the strength of character and the purpose to claim her. He can answer "her passionate glance of appeal" only with a "look of defeat and submission." After a time, her father in effect sells her to the highest bidder: he arranges a marriage for her with a man she has no interest in. Her fate is sealed hard work and a loveless marriage. Her love is to be thwarted by her father's interest in money. What would be natural and normal and good is defeated by economic obsessions which bring tragedy to the people most affected.

In "Galway Bay," another harshly drawn but moving vignette of peasant life, cantankerous, eighty-year-old Tom O'Donnell is bereft of his children (who have gone to America) and his wife (who is dead). One of his daughters comes back to Ireland ostensibly to take care of him, but a disagreement arises between the two over the management of the family farm. Although the daughter and her husband attempt to dominate the decrepit but independent old man, he still controls his destiny; he takes his cow to the Galway fair to sell the animal against his daughter's wishes. In his loneliness and isolation he continues to manage his own life and to defy anyone who attempts to dominate him or take advantage of him. He still finds consolation in the beauty of animals and boats, for all other solace has been taken from him.

O'Flaherty has etched this penetrating portrait of a man who never surrenders his individuality with marvelous use of description and dialogue. The character and condition of the aged Aran Islanders are captured in every detail. The terror and misery of the human condition is balanced by a spark of fire, or by a gesture of control, which makes old Tom a heroic figure in the most unheroic conditions possible.

Another short story which is among the best O'Flaherty has written in recent years is called simply "Life." "Life" portrays the relationship between a recently born infant and the elderly grandfather of the family. A doting, stooped, trembling, wisp of a man, the aged grandfather needs almost as much attention as the baby. He has to be taken from his bed every morning, has to be washed and dressed, and has even to be guided to the bathroom. At meals, his food has to be chopped into small pieces and fed to him. While there is joy in doing such tasks for the infant, only resentment exists when these duties are performed for the grandfather. The old man delightedly plays with the baby; but, as the infant grows stronger every day, the strength of the grandfather wanes and he soon dies. The situation of youth and age and the resulting contrasts are effectively caught and rendered. The complete cycle of life is caught in a few pages. He who was so lovely on the day of his marriage has now passed his life on to another—his grandson. Nature's endless round moves forward, and as one of the neighboring women stresses: "The longest journey from the womb to the grave is only a short one after all."[21] Such a story, built on such an obvious and basic comparison, could easily be trite; but so sharp and so stark is O'Flaherty's etching that the narrative takes on depth and universal significance, and the memory of this tale burns indelibly in the mind.

The most delightful story of O'Flaherty's later period, and a story most uncharacteristic of his career, is "The Post Office." Only on rare occasions does O'Flaherty evince a sense of humor throughout his writing career; and, when he does attempt to be light and whimsical, he generally fails to achieve these qualities. Yet in "The Post Office" he manages to be amusing and pleasant. Actually, the story is much more in the manner of Frank O'Connor than of Liam O'Flaherty.

The scene is a post office in a tiny seaside town in the remote regions of County Galway. Martin Conlon, the postmaster, is very much an individualist whose pet hate is sending telegrams. When three tourists request that a telegram be sent in Spanish, Martin is considerably distressed. He cannot legitimately refuse to send the wire, and the local people, knowing his attitude, gather around to watch his discomfiture. He must phone the message to Galway City, and in the process he undergoes considerable difficulty with a "comedy of errors" party line and the disconcerting aspects of "newfangled gadgets."

Conlon's various attempts to extricate himself from his dilemma— how can he be certain that the Spanish is not obscene, he inquires—are richly entertaining and yet plausible under the conditions of time and place. The garrulousness and yokel-like behavior of some of the natives also add expansiveness to the comedy. One of the old natives attempts to arrange a marriage match right on the spot, while an amazed aged crone inquires in all seriousness about a disease on the feet of the two women tourists—"The poor creatures must be rotting. Their toe-nails have turned red on them."[22]

In short, "The Post Office" is so genial and good-humored and is handled with such facility that we wonder why O'Flaherty has not written more in this vein and why he has waited so late in his career to assay a story of this nature. It is, of course, apparent that, while such a vein was within O'Flaherty, he has generally allowed his serious side to predominate in his fiction; nevertheless, more successful humorous stories would have broadened his creative range, produced more figures in the lovable vein of Thomsy Hynes, and have made O'Flaherty more appealing as a writer.

It should be noted that in 1953 O'Flaherty published *Dúil*, a collection of short stories in Gaelic. O'Flaherty wrote Gaelic stories in two periods, from 1924 to 1925 and from 1946 to 1952, but almost all of these tales have been issued in English versions. The most recent Gaelic stories, including the ones in *Dúil*, appear in English either in the *Two Lovely Beasts and Other Stories* volume or in *The Stories of Liam O'Flaherty* (1956). O'Flaherty's writing of Gaelic narratives has been lauded by several critics, but he preferred to write in English because he could reach a wider audience ("I chose the best language for presenting . . . ideas to my people. As the people spoke English I naturally wrote in English. If I wrote in Irish they would not be able to read" the material) and because of financial considerations. (He recalls, for example, that he and Pádraic Ó Conaire wanted to develop Gaelic language drama and organize a traveling theater, for which he offered to write ten plays. This proposal was not well received by the Gaeltacht Commission.) O'Flaherty did write one Gaelic play (*Darkness*) for which he received no payment. Such a situation would, therefore, discourage him from writing Gaelic plays and short stories except as a now-and-then pleasurable avocation.

O'Flaherty's most successful recent short stories such as "Two Lovely Beasts," "Galway Bay," and a lighthearted narrative such as "The Post Office" demonstrate that he can still, on occasion, summon considerable artistry in the genre of short fiction. In general, however, most of the more recent stories lack the gusto and verve of the earliest narratives; for O'Flaherty's work has become more subdued, more rambling, and less vivid. His recent animal stories, such as "The Water Hen" and "The Grey Seagull," are much less keenly presented and meaningful, less closely and freshly observed, than stories in a similar vein written in the earlier period. Many of the later stories are unreal and artificial, forced in plot, overly obvious in theme, and flat in effect. Less force and less beauty appear; and the surging waves of lyricism and emotion have, all too often, become tranquil and tame. The "fiery ecstasy" has subsided; and, for O'Flaherty's short fiction, this is indeed a misfortune.

### IV  *Final Estimate*

No sensible judgement of Liam O'Flaherty's literary work can result in either a wholly favorable or wholly unfavorable estimate. O'Flaherty's writing is characterized by some extremely worth-while attributes as well as by faults hardly commensurate with his natural genius. On the negative side, O'Flaherty's deficiencies can be epitomized. Much of his style is prosaic, heavy-handed, even clumsy, rather Dreiser-like—to name O'Flaherty's closest American counterpart—when he writes in his Naturalistic vein. Although O'Flaherty can be poetic and write exquisite passages when he chooses, he has a weakness for using flat language and the most frequently used clichés. He also has a decided tendency to overuse several words, such as "amazing" and "terrific."[23] His vocabulary, which appears relatively limited, often fails him; but, perhaps because of its narrow and often stilted nature, his dialogue unquestionably is an accurate reflection of common speech.

Like Dreiser, whom O'Flaherty professed to admire,[24] O'Flaherty is not at his best when it comes to moralizing and philosophizing. Too often his comments are overly obvious and rather jejune; they are jumbled, consist of mere rhetoric, and lack a depth of thought and knowledge which would raise them to a more meaningful level. The reflections rendered upon details observed fail, therefore, to equal the effectiveness of the accuracy of the observation. As George Russell once wrote about O'Flaherty, "He is a genius when he imagines and creates and a goose, a delightful goose, when he thinks and reasons."[25] Only seldom do O'Flaherty's attempts at philosophical speculation come to any level of success. On several occasions he avoids, as Frank O'Connor once observed, making reflections which would be useful and significant.[26] Sean O'Faolain's comment on this matter is extremely perceptive: "Since [O'Flaherty] is so much a Romantic one should not expect intellectual as well as emotional rewards from his work. I regret their absence—as I do in Hemingway: it is an equally pointless regret."[27]

Frank O'Connor's analysis of this aspect of O'Flaherty is also irrefutable:

When he describes the instinctual life of human beings—of children, women and men from his own wild countryside—there is no question in my mind that he writes as a master. He has all Lawrence's power of conveying the enchantment of the senses which is part of the instinctual life and, unlike Lawrence, does not romanticize or rationalize it. He begins to go false only when he has to deal with people who are compelled to live by their judgment rather than their instincts.[28]

Most of O'Flaherty's deficiencies in style and thought are caused by his lack of composure and artistic discipline. As a result, he appears to write down the first idea which comes into his head regardless of the total effect. Since he writes quickly, in a *furor poeticus,* the material is recorded in passionate outbursts. In most instances he uses the first and simplest words that come to his mind. In one of his letters to Edward Garnett, O'Flaherty claims to write without style since his creative energy would be thwarted by stylistic artificiality. Later in the same letter he retracts this statement and maintains he uttered such a comment in a moment of irritability. Nevertheless, O'Flaherty's original observation is more accurate than not. Lacking patience and discipline and possessing a natural indolence, O'Flaherty does not review or revise enough; he does not ponder the defects of his excitability and suddenly rushing thoughts. As a consequence, much that is trivial and second-rate intrudes in his writing; and these elements detract from sections which are much more inspired and artistic.

As thoughts come from his characters' minds without artistic control, the abrupt character whims and impulses become sharply inconsistent on many occasions. In such novels as *The Black Soul, Mr. Gilhooley, The Assassin*, and *The Puritan*, for example, so many contradictory impulses are emitted that at times the characters themselves seem incredible. The point is not that such contradictory thoughts, words, and impulses could not occur, but rather that, in the manner in which they are handled by O'Flaherty, they seem unnatural and improbable. He simply has not taken the time and care that, for example, Dostoevski did to develop these notions in a logical fashion. O'Flaherty has simply put down what has poured out, and he does not appear to realize that the conscious artist must shape and bring order out of chaos.

Another fault to which O'Flaherty is prone is his too-frequent tendency to explain his characters' actions in lengthy expository passages. Instead of letting his characters reveal themselves in dialogue or in action or allowing his expository and descriptive materials to blend cohesively, O'Flaherty often uses the old-fashioned expository-passage technique in which he baldly makes analytical comments about the characters' behavior. Not only does this method jar by being rough and elementary, it often causes the additional problem of not relating adequately to the narrative episode. In some instances the reader has figured out the reasons for the characters' actions before O'Flaherty gives his set explanation. On other occasions, the explanation is presented too soon; and much of the impact and suspense is therefore lost.

O'Flaherty's general success in a particular novel is contingent on whether or not he can make his characters consistent, credible, and memorable. Gypo Nolan, Connemara Maggie, Larry Gilhooley, the Kilmartins, Thomsy Hynes, and others are well conceived and presented. But all too often O'Flaherty's characters lack the depth and dimension which would render them more significant and thus render the novels—excluding *The Informer, Mr. Gilhooley*, and *Famine*—greater than they are. All too often he does not create fully imagined and credible people; as a result, there is a deficiency of character appeal in his work which leaves too many of the novels only half-satisfying. Too frequently O'Flaherty, instead of revealing his characters, "simply gives us," to quote the astute words of Mary Colum, "convincing information about [them]." O'Flaherty does not exhibit so often as he should the "power to reveal life, as against the power of describing it or making it interesting."[29]

Just as O'Flaherty's defects are glaringly apparent, so are most of his virtues. He is, first of all, an expert at handling narrative interest. His ability as a story teller and the imaginative power often observed in his work extenuate, to a degree, some of his most obvious flaws. Action, too, is one of his strong points; he can usually make even the most incredible action or event persuasive and suspenseful. He "can invent most Irish writers off the map."[30] And J. B. Priestley remarks, "O'Flaherty has that which will atone for a thousand faults in his manner; he has imagination, unifying his story and driving it forward, and the reader with it. He has the seeing eye; he believes in the narrative he has to tell, and, incredible as it may all appear after sober reflection, he makes us believe it too."[31] Or, to put it in Yeats's terms, when he was comparing George Moore to O'Flaherty: "He joyously *imagines* where Moore *constructs* and yet is more real than Moore."[32]

Furthermore, O'Flaherty possesses the innate ability to write pictorially, so that such elements as color, sound, and concrete-scene impressions are communicated in an accomplished manner. Mary Colum records that O'Flaherty's "observation is sound, his facts are accurate, and he has an intimate knowledge of the Irish people and their attitude of mind";[33] and Horace Reynolds believes that "No one—not even Synge—has written better of the Irish peasant of the West, struggling with harsh land and bitter sea."[34] This comment does not mean, however, that O'Flaherty can rival Synge in style. As Vivian Mercier has pointed out, O'Flaherty, because of his temperament, "writes far more for the eye than he does for the ear or the speaking voice."[35] O'Flaherty views his scenes and people with a camera eye,

and very few writers possess greater ability to make us "see."
O'Flaherty can thus surpass Synge on a visual level, yet Synge is far
more lyrical and poetic. "The reader [of O'Flaherty]," Mercier
observes, "will search in vain for the cadences which Synge put into the
mouths" of his Aran Islanders.[36]

On occasion, O'Flaherty can also bring to his writing levels of poetic
mysticism, gusto, and excitement which give his stories a basic
enchantment and an aura of hypnotizing fury. O'Flaherty infuses much
of his writing with an intense energy that wells up "in a sort of wild and
untired wave . . . in a sort of delirium that transcends reason."[37] He has
an avid thirst for violence. Both O'Flaherty and his protagonists are
usually straining at the limitations of existence, and there floods
through O'Flaherty's work a promethean gusto, a clinched fist-shaking
defiance at the gods. The exuberant hurricane of excitement sweeps to
heights of struggle and turmoil which induce a trance in the reader. The
concluding sections of *Thy Neighbour's Wife* and *Mr. Gilhooley*, the
wild fumbling of Gypo Nolan after his act of treachery, the anguish and
agonies found in *The Black Soul, The Assassin*, and *The Puritan* could
have been produced only by a natural genius, who often can "storm the
highest heavens." George Russell said in reviewing *The Black Soul* that
O'Flaherty had written "the most elemental thing in modern Irish
literature." This phrase applies to most of O'Flaherty's novels, and they
are still the most elemental works in modern Irish literature.

O'Flaherty's novels always deal with significant themes. He records
man's incessant struggles to be more than he is—to be, in actuality, a
god, "to be free from death and the restraint of the earth's balance."[38]
O'Flaherty relates the turmoil of man's unhappiness with his condition,
his desires for knowledge, and his "being constantly in revolt." In
dealing, too, with the "Prudery, Hypocrisy, Deceit, Opportunism,
Political Guile, Moral Cowardice"[39] found in the people he describes,
O'Flaherty has proved to be a crusader and a champion for common
sense and enlightenment. Although he has encountered a vast amount
of censorship, personal attacks, and abuse in Ireland, he can write
touchingly and meaningfully: "I claim that Ireland is the only country
where I feel of any consequence as a writer. It is the only country
where I feel the youth and freshness of Spring among the people, where
I feel at one with my mates, where I sing with their singing and weep
with their weeping."[40] Not the least appealing quality of O'Flaherty's
work is the fact that he is continually distressed with things which, or
people who, in Yeats's lines, wrong "the image that blossoms a rose in
the deeps of the heart."

Some comment is required about the general neglect of O'Flaherty by literary critics. O'Flaherty is one of the significant Irish writers—Sean O'Faolain, Frank O'Connor, Mary Lavin, and Paul Vincent Carroll are some others—who have been pushed into the background because of the Irish Big Four syndrome that afflicts critics. Synge, Yeats, O'Casey, and Joyce have drawn so much attention that other important Anglo-Irish authors have either been neglected or unduly denigrated.

O'Flaherty must share much of the blame for his own critical neglect since he has taken every opportunity to censure, discourage, and mislead literary critics who might otherwise have given him a more complete hearing and might have been less inclined to judge him on the basis of his weakest books and his oral denunciations. Enraged that his first two novels did not receive the favorable critical reception he deemed them worthy of, O'Flaherty turned on the critics when they enthusiastically received *The Informer*. He then attempted to show how the critics had been easily deceived and erroneous about a book that he claimed to have written primarily as a prank.

O'Flaherty's overemphasis on the money motif for writers—some of this attitude being a pose and some of it again being a sneer at critics—also caused loss of critical prestige. Furthermore, O'Flaherty has too frequently with active belligerence met critical generosity or fair-minded attempts to analyze his work. Much evidence exists to support the theory that an ingrown sense of contrariness is forever active in O'Flaherty's makeup—some of the Samuel Johnson quality of taking the opposite side of an issue just for the sake of an argument also is present. O'Flaherty seems to enjoy a martyrdom complex. When he calls himself the "most unpopular man in Ireland," he takes a certain pleasure in this claim.

One final matter that needs comment concerns O'Flaherty's classification as a Naturalist or a Romantic. It is apparent that Naturalism occurs in O'Flaherty's work, and he professed to be an admirer of Zola.[41] The documentary nature of much of his material, the stress on brutality and squalor in slum environments, the emphasis on examining closely the impoverished, the unbalanced, the seriously disturbed, the authenticity and multiplicity of his descriptive details—these and similar aspects are Naturalistic. The philosophy of Naturalism in which man is presented as a helpless victim can be observed in several of O'Flaherty's books. Man is depicted as the victim of forces outside and inside—environment, passions, heredity.

Yet at other times, O'Flaherty holds out some hope for man, and very much in the manner of some American writers, for instance, Frank

Norris and Jack London, O'Flaherty combines Naturalistic and Romantic qualities.

Sean O'Faolain says that O'Flaherty is primarily "an inverted romantic. That is, he sets out in the most self-conscious and deliberate way to attack with violence the things that hurt the inarticulated dream of his romantic soul . . . he has the inflated ego of the romantic, the dissatisfaction of the romantic, the wild imagination, the response to the magic of nature, the self-pity of the romantic, his masochistic rage, the unbalance." [42] O'Faolain notes that O'Flaherty's work is frequently dominated by hate; the writing wells up with *saeva indignatio.* This disgust, which is not uncommon in O'Flaherty's attitude toward the peasants, for example, is not characteristic of most Naturalistic writers although it motivated some of them. [43] Yet at the same time O'Flaherty is not a thoroughgoing Romantic since he sees much more than his dream—he also records the bitterness of reality. In essence, he never reconciles the common Irish conflict between Romantic dreaming and harsh reality. He never grows out of Romanticism, yet he is too much of a Naturalist to give his allegiance completely to his emotionalism and subjectivism. That O'Flaherty never came to harmonize these two diverse elements in his personality and in his literary work is, above all, the mark of his success and the measure of his failure.

# Notes and References

*Preface*

1. Sean O'Faolain, "Fifty Years of Irish Writing," *Studies*, LI (Spring, 1962), 102.

*Chapter One*

1. According to O'Flaherty, the film did not present a true picture of the life of the people; see Gault MacGowan, "Girls Mature Before Boys," *New York Evening Sun*, December 6, 1937.
2. John Millington Synge, *The Aran Islands* (Boston, n. d.), p. 65.
3. *Ibid.*, p. 60. See also P. A. O Siochain, *Aran: Islands of Legend* (New York, 1962).
4. *Skerrett* (New York, 1932), pp. 126-27.
5. *Joseph Conrad: An Appreciation* (London, 1930), p. 11.
6. *A Tourist's Guide to Ireland* (London, 1929), p. 16.
7. *Ibid.*, pp. 75-76.
8. Liam O'Flaherty, "Autobiographical Note," *Ten Contemporaries, Second Series*, ed. John Gawsworth (London, 1933), p. 139.
9. O'Flaherty first came to Rockwell in September, 1908 and left there in July, 1913. He passed the Junior Grade State Examination in 1909 with Honors in Greek, Latin, and French. In the Middle Grade Examination he won First Class Exhibitions in Classics and modern languages gaining money prizes in both groups and won money prizes as well for his Latin and Irish compositions. In the Middle Grade Examination in 1912 he won First Class Exhibitions in modern languages and Classics and was second in the country in his marks for modern languages and fifth (in Ireland) in his Greek and Latin marks. Again, he won money prizes; personal communication to the present writer from Reverend William A. Gardiner of Rockwell College, July 6, 1966. O'Flaherty later noted his scholastic success at Rockwell, but in retrospect claimed to have disliked the school for its alleged "melancholy attitude." However, he did acknowledge the help and enthusiasm of a "brilliant priest" there, Father Mahoney, who encouraged him in

writing and in his studies, Liam O'Flaherty, "My Life of Adventure," *TP's Weekly*, X (October 20, 1928), 756. Much of the same autobiographical material in this article is repeated in O'Flaherty's "My Experiences (1896–1923)," *Now and Then*, No. 10 (December, 1923), pp. 14–15.

10. O'Flaherty entered Blackrock as a boarding student at the beginning of September, 1913. In June, 1914, he presented himself for the Senior Grade Examination of the Intermediate Board of Education for Ireland. He obtained honors marks in Greek, Latin, English, history and geography, and Irish; pass marks in mathematics. He qualified for the award of an "Exhibition" of £30 in each of two groups of subjects: Group A (Latin and Greek) and Group B (two subjects from French, German, Irish, Latin). Only one award could be taken by a student, and he was given the "Exhibition" for his marks in Irish and Latin, being ranked first among the students of Group B throughout the country. His rank in Group A was fifth. O'Flaherty left Blackrock in June, 1914; personal communication to the present writer from Reverend John Ryan, Blackrock College, June 4, 1966.

11. O'Flaherty entered Holy Cross College, Clonliffe, on September 28, 1914. He entered the First Arts Class at University College, Dublin, where Holy Cross students do their Philosophical Degree work. O'Flaherty left Clonliffe on November 18, 1914; personal communication to the present writer from Reverend J. A. Carroll, president of Holy Cross College, June 6, 1966. During 1914–15, O'Flaherty held an Entrance Scholarship in Classics. In 1915, he passed First Arts and was awarded a Second Class Exhibition. He was granted the B.A. degree (War) in 1918; personal communication to the present writer from Thomas Murphy, Registrar of University College, June 4, 1966.

12. *New York Evening Post*, October 4, 1930, p. 4. Further, a boasting quality of Irish storytelling and romanticizing is typical of O'Flaherty. He himself parodies this characteristic in one of his novels—*The Black Soul* (New York, 1925), pp. 53-54—when he presents three men drinking in a tavern and, amusingly, has each try to out-boast the other. "It seemed," remarks O'Flaherty, "that the three of them had spent all their lives fighting, drinking, and breaking women's hearts."

13. *Shame the Devil* (London, 1934), pp. 20–21.

14. *Ibid.*, p. 21. One version indicates that for a time O'Flaherty considered becoming a missionary to native Africans.

15. *Ibid.: Ten Contemporaries*, p. 141; personal communication to the present writer from Reverend William A. Gardiner of Rockwell College, July 6, 1966.

16. *Ten Contemporaries*, p. 141. He repeats this version in "My Life of Adventure," *TP's Weekly*, X (October 20, 1928), 756: "In 1915 I got tired waiting for an Irish revolution and I joined the Irish Guards."

17. *Two Years* (London, 1930), p. 151.

18. A priest who taught O'Flaherty at Rockwell reported that O'Flaherty neglected his medical studies and joined the army so he would not lose his scholarship; reported in a communication to the present writer from Reverend William A. Gardiner of Rockwell College, July 6, 1966. That this view is accurate could be surmised by the seemingly autobiographical statement about the year of debauch the protagonist of *The Black Soul* participated in before he joined the army; *The Black Soul*, p. 32.

19. Another explanation—seemingly unlikely—offered is that, when the church hierarchy of Ireland urged the people to save Catholic Belgium, O'Flaherty heeded the appeal and joined the British Army, *Living Authors*, ed. Dilly Tante (New York, 1931), p. 305.

20. *Ten Contemporaries*, p. 141; *Shame the Devil*, p. 21. Although all the standard accounts of O'Flaherty's life state that he was wounded at Langemarck, the dust jackets of both the English and American editions of *The Return of the Brute* assert that he was wounded at Passchendaele (now spelled Passendale), a village in western Belgium.

21. Related rather sketchily in *Two Years*.

22. *Two Years*, p. 300.

23. *Shame the Devil*, p. 22.

24. Gerald Griffin, *The Wild Geese: Pen Portraits of Famous Irish Exiles* (London, 1938), p. 192.

25. *Ibid.*

26. *Ten Contemporaries*, p. 141.

27. See P. M. Esslinger, "The Irish Alienation of Sean O'Casey," *Eire—Ireland*, I (Spring, 1965–66), 18–25. Cf. also O'Flaherty's *A Tourist's Guide to Ireland*.

28. "Irish Housekeeping," *New Statesman and Nation*, XI (February 8, 1936), 186.

29. *Authors Take Sides on the Spanish War* (London, 1937), n.p.

30. "Fascism or Communism," *The Irish Statesman*, VI (May 8, 1926), 231–32.

31. *New York Times*, February 9, 1940, p. 8.

32. During the early period of Castro's establishment of a Communist satellite in Cuba, O'Flaherty met a University College, Dublin, professor and lauded Castro's action with considerable enthusiasm. Not so long thereafter, O'Flaherty again encountered the same professor and expressed completely opposite sentiments about Castro. This anecdote tends to confirm the inconsistency of O'Flaherty's thought. His bent has always been toward political radicalness, but he has not worried about consistency of viewpoint. But we should perhaps remember that O'Flaherty could change his views after he learned more facts, and perhaps also Emerson's remark about consistency should be recalled.

33. *Shame the Devil*, p. 22.

34. *Ibid.*, p. 23.

35. *Ibid.*, p. 38.

36. Comments by O'Flaherty quoted on the dust jacket of the first British edition of *Thy Neighbour's Wife* (London, 1923).

37. The dependence of O'Flaherty upon Garnett, particularly during this period, can be best observed by reading O'Flaherty's well over one hundred letters and postcards written to his editor. These epistles are preserved at the Academic Center Library of the University of Texas. They demonstrate the fact that O'Flaherty was writing much of his work at this time to please his closest friend. Another indication of this friendship is the fact that O'Flaherty was one of the witnesses to Garnett's will, H. E. Bates, *Edward Garnett* (London, 1950), p. 46.

38. Sean O'Casey, *Inishfallen, Fare Thee Well* (New York, 1949), pp. 169—71, 371.

39. *Two Years*, pp. 218—19.

40. *Shame the Devil*, p. 284.

41. *Ibid.*, p. 285.

42. *Ibid.*, p. 103.

43. *Two Years*, p. 219.

44. *Living Authors*, p. 306.

45. Edwin Muir, *Transition* (New York, 1926), pp. 49, 51.

46. *Thy Neighbour's Wife* (New York, 1924), pp. 122—23.

47. *Ibid.*, p. 259.

48. *Ibid.*, p. 133.

49. *Ibid.*, p. 314.

50. *Ibid.*, p. 315.

51. *Ibid.*, p. 336.

52. *Ibid.*, p. 196.

53. *Spectator*, CXXXII (May 17, 1924), 809.

54. *Thy Neighbour's Wife*, p. 31.

55. *The Aran Islands*, pp. 96-97.

56. *The Black Soul*, p. 33.

57. O'Flaherty paid particular tribute to Garnett in *Ten Contemporaries*, p. 143. There are over 160 pieces of correspondence from O'Flaherty to Garnett now catalogued at the Humanities Research Center of the University of Texas.

58. *The Black Soul*, p. 132.

59. *Ibid.*, p. 133.

60. *Ibid.*, pp. 185—86.

61. *Ibid.*, p. 247.

62. O'Flaherty testifies to the accuracy of the geographical description in a letter to Edward Garnett, April 27, 1924.

63. AE's review of *The Black Soul, The Irish Statesman*, II (May 3, 1924), 244. Also reprinted in *Now and Then*, No. 12 (Summer, 1924),

pp. 26–27. In a letter written to Edward Garnett on April 27, 1924, O'Flaherty claims that AE remarked that *The Black Soul* was the finest book ever produced by an Irish writer. This letter is part of the Academic Center Library collection at the University of Texas.

64. "National Energy," *The Irish Statesman*, III (October 18, 1924), 171. In a letter to Edward Garnett, written in April, 1924, O'Flaherty asserts that a writer must possess "spiritual ecstasy" in order to pursue his belief in a book that he is writing.

65. In a letter excerpted and summarized in a University of Texas library catalogue, O'Flaherty expresses his belief that Primitivism as a trend will increase, *A Creative Century: An Exhibition–Selections from the Twentieth Century Collections at the University of Texas* (Austin, 1964), p. 46.

66. J. B. Priestley, review of *The Black Soul*, *London Mercury*, X (July, 1924), 212.

### Chapter Two

1. Donagh MacDonagh, "Afterword," *The Informer* (New York, 1961), p. 184.

2. *Ibid.*, p. 185.

3. *Ibid.*, pp. 133–34.

4. *Ibid.*, p. 69.

5. *Ibid.*, pp. 73–74.

6. *Ibid.*, p. 71.

7. *Ibid.*, p. 107.

8. Vivian Mercier, "The Irish Short Story and Oral Tradition," *The Celtic Cross: Studies in Irish Culture and Literature*, ed. R. B. Browne, William J. Roscelli, and Richard Loftus (Lafayette, Indiana, 1964), p. 105. There is an excellent monograph on the Gaelic oral tradition by J. H. Delargy, *The Gaelic Story-Teller with Some Notes on Gaelic Folk-Tales* (Chicago, 1969).

9. O'Flaherty indicates his satisfaction with *The Black Soul* as opposed to *The Informer* in a letter to Edward Garnett written on January 20, 1925.

10. *Ten Contemporaries*, p. 143.

11. *Shame the Devil*, p. 191.

12. *Ibid.*, p. 190.

13. *Ibid.*, pp. 187–88, 190–91.

14. Letter to Edward Garnett, dated April 1924, Academic Center Library, University of Texas.

15. Letter to Edward Garnett, dated July 28, 1924, Academic Center Library, University of Texas.

16. The screen version was written by Dudley Nichols. The scenario may be found in *Theatre Arts*, XXXV (August, 1951), 60–82. It

should be noted that the "Cutting Continuity" version of the movie is printed by Harlan Hatcher in his collection, *Modern British Drama* (New York, 1941), pp. 297–367, and in his *Modern Drama*, Shorter Edition (New York, 1944), pp. 199–265. Lewis Jacobs in his *The Rise of the American Film: A Critical History* (New York, 1939) makes several perceptive remarks about the effectiveness of the movie, pp. 480–83. The impact made by *The Informer* is further indicated by Jules Dassin's movie *Up Tight*, which, using the plot of *The Informer* as a basis, transfers the scene to Cleveland in 1968, shortly after the assassination of the Reverend Martin Luther King, Jr. A group of black militants kill one of their number, Tank, who informs. The story, setting, and memorableness of Tank as a character, however, do not approach the beautifully balanced and interwoven relationship found among these three ingredients in John Ford's film or in the original O'Flaherty novel.

17. William Troy, "The Position of Liam O'Flaherty," *The Bookman* (New York), LXIX (March, 1929), 9.

### Chapter Three

1. Vivian Mercier, "Introduction," *The Stories of Liam O'Flaherty* (New York 1956), p. viii.

2. *The Stories of Liam O'Flaherty*, p. 68.

3. *Modern Irish Short Stories*, ed. Frank O'Connor (London, 1957), p. xii.

4. *The Stories of Liam O'Flaherty*, p. 191.

5. *Ibid.*, p. 197.

6. *The Aran Islands.*, p. 64.

7. *The Stories of Liam O'Flaherty*, p. 23.

8. *Ibid.*, p. 25.

9. *Ibid.*, p. 38.

10. *Ibid.*, p. 32.

11. This interpretation is confirmed by O'Flaherty in a letter, written on June 23, 1926, that is now part of the Fales Collection at New York University Library.

12. Sean O'Faolain, *Vive Moi!* (Boston, 1964), p. 339.

13. *Ten Contemporaries*, p. 143.

14. *The Aran Islands*, p. 62.

15. Frank O'Connor, "A Good Story Must Be News," *New York Times Book Review*, June 10, 1956, Section 7, p. 20.

16. In a letter written to a Mr. Spohn in 1926, O'Flaherty calls this story, "the best thing I have done." This letter is in the present writer's collection of O'Flaherty letters.

17. *The Stories of Liam O'Flaherty*, p. 110.

18. Sean O'Faolain, "Don Quixote O'Flaherty," *The Bell*, II (June, 1941). 35.

19. Review of *Spring Sowing, New York Times,* July 4, 1926, p. 6.

20. George Brandon Saul, "A Wild Sowing: The Short Stories of Liam O'Flaherty," *A Review of English Literature,* IV (July, 1963), 109.

21. "A Good Story Must Be News," p. 1.

22. Horace Reynolds, review of *Two Lovely Beasts and Other Stories, New York Times,* July 16, 1950, p. 4.

23. Bates, *Edward Garnett,* p. 47.

24. Muir, p. 49.

25. Frank O'Connor, *The Lonely Voice: A Study of the Short Story* (Cleveland and New York, 1963), p. 27.

26. "A Good Story Must Be News," p. 20.

27. "Don Quixote O'Flaherty," *The Bell,* II (June, 1941), 35.

28. "The Position of Liam O'Flaherty," p. 7.

### Chapter Four

1. "The Position of Liam O'Flaherty," p. 8.

2. Lillian Hellman, "Introduction," *Six Plays by Lillian Hellman* (New York, 1960), p. xii.

3. MacDonagh, pp. 187–88.

4. *Ibid.;* MacDonagh notes that the window presentation was never made since it was felt that such figures as Gilhooley and Leopold Bloom would not be worthy representatives of Irish life.

5. Yeats also believed that *The Informer* was a "great" book; *The Letters of W. B. Yeats,* ed. Allan Wade (New York, 1955), p. 722. Also found in Joseph Hone, *William Butler Yeats 1865–1939,* Second Edition (London, 1965), p. 380.

6. Convenient reviews of Elser's dramatization "Mr. Gilhooley" may be found in *Commonweal,* XII (October 15, 1930), 610, and in the *Catholic World,* CXXXII (November, 1930), 206–7.

7. Liam O'Flaherty, *Mr. Gilhooley* (London, 1926), p. 7. All quotations from this novel are taken from the first unexpurgated British edition.

8. *Ibid.,* p. 23.

9. *Ibid.,* p. 30.

10. *Ibid.,* p. 105.

11. *Ibid.,* pp. 145–46.

12. *Ibid.,* pp. 165–66.

13. Cf. the British edition of *Mr. Gilhooley,* p. 242, and the American edition (New York, 1927), p. 237.

14. Cf. British edition, p. 252, and the American edition, p. 247.

15. Cf. British edition, p. 245, and the American edition. p. 240.

16. In one of his emotionally outspoken moods, O'Flaherty suggested that women throughout the world should be eliminated. In the same breath, he also declared that New York City and Hollywood

should be destroyed, Robert Ruark, "Signs of the Times," *New York World Telegram*, April 8, 1947.

17. For an account of O'Higgins's career and assassination, see Terence de Vere White, *Kevin O'Higgins* (London, 1948).

18. *The Assassin* (New York, 1928), p. 202.

19. O'Flaherty is able to inject much intense realism in his work because he personally has experienced much of what occurs in his novels, or he has been close enough to his literary material to imagine with accuracy the thoughts and emotions of his characters. In one of his nonfictional works he relates how he vividly experienced a "mania of being pursued by assassins"; and he waited, revolver in hand, for their arrival, *Shame the Devil*, p. 41.

20. See, for example, William York Tindall, *Forces in Modern British Literature 1885–1946* (New York, 1947), p. 99. Tindall omits the reference to O'Flaherty's commercial intentions in the 1956 revised edition of the book.

21. *Shame the Devil*, pp. 39–40.

22. *Ibid.*, p. 44.

23. *Ibid.*, p. 187.

24. *Ibid.*, pp. 189–90.

25. *Ibid.*, p. 244.

26. "Writing in Gaelic," *The Irish Statesman*, IX (December 17, 1927), 348.

27. In his letters to Garnett he indicates that he attempts to write pure art but at times he complains that he must compose too hastily for financial reasons. Note the severe money problems O'Flaherty faced as mentioned in a letter to Edward Garnett, January 24, 1926, now a part of the Academic Center Library collection at the University of Texas.

28. *I Went to Russia* (London, 1931), p. 11.

29. *Ibid.*, p. 51.

30. *Shame the Devil*, p. 239.

31. *I Went to Russia*, p. 25.

32. *The Life of Tim Healy* (New York, 1927), p. 8

33. *Two Years*, p. 14. An interesting letter in the O'Flaherty materials (Fales Collection at New York University Library) indicates O'Flaherty's indolence in regard to writing and records how his wife forces him to write by nagging and pestering him.

34. Some critics have found *The House of Gold* effective. Frank Swinnerton, for example, lauds its vividness, suspensefulness, and poetic eloquence, "Liam O'Flaherty's New Novel," *Now and Then*, No. 34 (Winter, 1929), pp. 28–29.

35. Chester Erskin adapted a version of *The Puritan* for the New York stage.

36. In the November 1, 1930, issue of the *New York Times* it is reported that the first book by an Irish author banned under the new

censorship act was one of O'Flaherty's novels, *The House of Gold. The Puritan* was also banned in Ireland for obscenity, although the *New York Times* pointed out in its "Book Notes" column on March 19, 1932, that William Butler Yeats had written to the *Manchester Guardian* and protested against this censorship, calling *The Puritan* "a great book." *The Puritan* was made into a movie in Paris; but, before this picture could be shown in New York City, it was banned by the New York State Board of Censors.

37. Quoted from an interview with O'Flaherty by Gault MacGowan, "Girls Mature Before Boys," *New York Evening Sun*, December 6, 1937.

38. *The Puritan* (New York, 1932), p. 81.

39. *Ibid.*, pp. 190–91.

40. *Ibid.*, p. 313.

41. *Two Years*, pp. 216–17.

42. *I Went to Russia*, p. 138. Yet O'Flaherty's essentially protean attitudes and on-again, off-again caprices can be again observed when he ridicules Dostoevski while reviewing a novel by Ethel Mannin: "The chronicle is not disfigured by any . . . tension of the kind that makes Dostoevski fit only for intimates of lunatic asylums," *The Irish Statesman*, VI (June 5, 1926), 360.

43. Benedict Kiely, *Modern Irish Fiction—A Critique* (Dublin, 1950), p. 18.

44. *I Went to Russia*, p. 58.

45. O'Flaherty's successful *Famine* is not included in this statement because it is not one of his "melodrama of the soul" novels.

46. For example, Mercier, "Introduction," *The Stories of Liam O'Flaherty*, p. vi; MacDonagh, "Afterword," *The Informer*, p. 188; O'Faolain, "Don Quixote O'Flaherty," *The Bell*, II (June, 1941), 33–34.

47. *Skerrett*, p. 274.

48. *Ibid.*

49. *Ibid.*, pp. 151–52.

50. *Ibid.*, p. 176.

51. *Ibid.*, pp. 56–57.

52. O'Faolain, "Don Quixote O'Flaherty," *The Bell*, pp. 33–34.

53. *Joseph Conrad: An Appreciation*, p. 7. In the Fales Collection at New York University Library, an unpublished fragment in O'Flaherty's hand indicates his striving for the secret of the universe, which is within one's self and constantly drives man forward in quest.

54. *Skerrett*, p. 246.

55. *Ibid.*, p. 146.

56. *Ibid.*, pp. 177–78.

57. *Ibid.*, p. 270.

58. *The Martyr* (New York, 1933), p. 66.

59. *Ibid.*, p. 169.

60. *The Letters of W. B. Yeats*, p. 809.

61. William Troy, "Mr. O'Flaherty's Development," *Nation*, CXXXVII (August 9, 1933), 165.

62. Basil Davenport, "Controlled Violence," *Saturday Review of Literature*, IX (June 10, 1933), 641.

63. *New Statesman and Nation*, V (January 21, 1933), 76.

*Chapter Five*

1. Cecil Woodham Smith, *The Great Hunger* (New York and Evanston, 1962), p. 285.

2. Mrs. Woodham Smith discusses the two separate diseases to which the people gave the name "famine fever," pp. 188–89.

3. *Famine* (New York, 1937), p. 268.

4. O'Flaherty's more customary attitude toward the "gombeen man" can be observed in *A Tourist's Guide to Ireland*.

5. *Ibid.*, p. 342.

6. *Ibid.*, p. 407. We might consider the pejorative connotation of "mitred felons" balanced somewhat by the more objective "gallant priest" reference mentioned in connection with the Wexford insurrection, p. 122.

7. R. M. Henry, *The Evolution of Sinn Fein* (New York, 1920), p. 304.

8. *Famine*, p. 338.

9. John V. Kelleher, "Irish Literature Today," *Atlantic Monthly*, CLXXV (March, 1945), 75.

10. N. L. Rothman, "Tragedy of Hunger," *Saturday Review of Literature*, XVI (October 2, 1937), 6.

11. "Don Quixote O'Flaherty," *The London Mercury*, p. 174.

12. Horace Reynolds, "Liam O'Flaherty's New Novel," *New York Times Book Review*, October 3, 1937, Sect. 7, p. 6.

13. In late 1937, O'Flaherty was reported to be working on a novel called *The Sun*. This novel was intended to contrast the amours of the Caribbean area with the affections characteristic of Ireland. The novel was to be called *The Sun* in opposition to O'Flaherty's novel of gloom (*Famine*), *New York Times*, November 23, 1937, "Book Notes"; Gault MacGowan, "Girls Mature Before Boys," *New York Evening Sun*, December 6, 1937.

14. The *New York Times* reported on October 8, 1952, that O'Flaherty and Walter Macken had completed a dramatic version of *The Informer*; but this play has not as yet been given a professional performance. Padraic and Delia O'Hehir note that O'Flaherty also wrote a play for the actor Micheál Mac Liammóir, cofounder of the Gate Theatre. This play was never produced. The information from the

O'Hehirs comes from interviews with them on June 24–25, 27–28, 1969. For much more than a decade, O'Flaherty has been creatively inactive. He has published no fiction since the mid–1950's. Of course, many of his early stories continue to be reprinted in anthologies and collections, and, now and then, something bibliographically unusual will appear; e.g., the story "His First Flight," *Ireland of the Welcomes*, XVII (March–April, 1969), 32–39, apparently received its first magazine publication on this date although it was printed in the *Spring Sowing* collection. According to Padraic and Delia O'Hehir, O'Flaherty retired from writing in order to live on his royalties and to enjoy leisure and traveling. Doubtless, too, the creative process had slowed with the onset of old age. An allegedly new story published by him in *Winter's Tales 6*, ed. A. D. Maclean (New York, 1960), proved to be "The Post Office," which had appeared previously in *The Bell* in April, 1954.

It should be noted that O'Flaherty published *Dúil*, a collection of short stories in Gaelic in 1953. After being absent from Eire for many years O'Flaherty returned in 1946 and urged a return to compulsory Irish: "I would go so far as to forbid the speaking of English altogether for ten years. I would make Irish as compulsory as English was in 1848," "Irish Revival Delights Liam O'Flaherty," *The Irish Press*, May 13, 1946, p. 4. It has been difficult to ascertain with complete certainty which stories O'Flaherty wrote first in Gaelic or first in English. As Tomas De Bhaldraithe records (Ó Flaithearta—Aistritheoir [O'Flaherty—Translator]," *Comhar*, XXVI [Bealtaine (May), 1967], 35–37), O'Flaherty wrote Gaelic stories in two periods, 1924–25 and 1946–52.

Since O'Flaherty has been reluctant to give information, we must rely on the list supplied by Padraic and Delia O'Hehir. According to the O'Hehirs, the following stories were first writtin in Gaelic: "Dúil," "An Charraig Dhubh," "An Buille," "An Chearc Uisce," "An Chulaith Nua," "An Luchóg," "Teangabháil," and "Uisce Faoi Dhráiocht." These stories were first written in English: "Bás na Bó," "An Faich," "Daoine Bochta," "An Taonaċ," "An Seabhac," "An Scáthán," "An Beo," "Díoltas," and "Oifig An Phoist." Information gathered from interviews with the O'Hehir family, June 24–25, 27–28, 1969.

De Bhaldraithe's test of comparing the flavor and style of the Gaelic version with the English version in order to determine the language in which the story was first written is extremely helpful. Thus "Teangabháil [The Touch]," and "An Chulaith Nua [The New Suit]"—which appear in the collection *Two Lovely Beasts and Other Stories* (1948)—were, as De Bhaldraithe theorizes, apparently first written in Gaelic. Almost all of O'Flaherty's stories written in Gaelic appear in English versions in the *Two Lovely Beasts* collection, in *The Stories of Liam O'Flaherty* (1956), and in the early short-story collections. A list of the magazine appearances of the stories may be found in P. A. Doyle's "A Liam O'Flaherty Checklist," *Twentieth Century Literature*, XIII (April, 1967), 50–51. This list is published and supplemented in the primary bibliography of this present critique. It is doubtful that a definitive bibliography of O'Flaherty's contributions to periodicals and newspapers can ever be compiled. This situation is particularly true of his writing in the 1920's. In many instances, no records of such writings were kept either by O'Flaherty or his literary agent; further, he contributed to an unusually large number of magazines of various types. Many of these periodicals are obscure, and many became defunct after publishing only a few issues. O'Flaherty also occasionally changed titles, so that the manuscript story is difficult to trace in published form. The fact, too, that many of the short stories he mentions in his correspondence were never published adds to the difficulty.

15. Sean O'Faolain, *The Irish: A Character Study* (New York, 1949). See especially pp. 129–55.

16. O'Flaherty believes that *Land* is "more virile than *Famine* and has more exciting situations," *The Irish Press*, May 13, 1946, p. 4.

17. Ascertained from interviews with Delia and Padraic O'Hehir, June 24–25, 27–28, 1969. In an interview with *The Irish Press*, May 13, 1946, p. 4, O'Flaherty claimed to have no favorite among his novels.

18. Related by the O'Hehirs, June 24–25, 27–28, 1969.

19. Walter Kerr, "Books," *Commonweal*, LIV (May 25, 1951), 171.

20. *Two Lovely Beasts and Other Stories* (New York, 1950), p. 15.

21. *Ibid.*, p. 250.

22. *Ibid.*, p. 392.

23. O'Faolain, in particular, stresses O'Flaherty's use of these adjectives, "Don Quixote O'Flaherty," *The Bell*, pp. 30–31.

24. *Living Authors*, p. 306.

25. *Letters from AE*, ed. Alan Denson (London, 1961), p. 172.

26. *Modern Irish Short Stories*, p. xii.

27. "Fifty Years of Irish Writing," p. 103.

28. "A Good Short Story Must Be News," p. 1.

29. Mary M. Colum, "Some New Irish Novelists," *New Republic*, XXXIX (July 2, 1924), 164.

30. F. MacM, "Novel of Land War," *The Irish Press*, July 11, 1946, p. 7.

31. Priestley, p. 212.

32. *The Letters of W. B. Yeats*, p. 722.

33. Colum, p. 164.

34. Horace Reynolds, review of *Two Lovely Beasts and Other Stories*, p. 4.

35. *The Celtic Cross*, p. 105.

36. *Ibid.*, p. 106.

37. Henry L. Stuart is speaking specifically about *Mr. Gilhooley*, but O'Flaherty's "melodrama of the soul" novels possess these qualities, *New York Times*, February 13, 1927, p. 12.

38. *Joseph Conrad: An Appreciation*, p. 7.

39. "Don Quixote O'Flaherty," *The Bell,* p. 28.

40. "The Irish Censorship," *The American Spectator*, I (November, 1932), 2.

41. Interviews with the O'Hehir family. They also noted that O'Flaherty professed much admiration for the work of Dostoevski, Turgenev, and the Gaelic author Pádraic Ó Conaire, with whom he was on cordial terms.

42. "Don Quixote O'Flaherty," *The Bell*, p. 34.

43. O'Flaherty believes that the world "can be changed by the hand of man into a paradise of happiness, with the aid of science, culture and power over the forces of nature," *The Life of Tim Healy*, p. 29. Such sentiments are not typical of a Naturalist.

# Selected Bibliography

## PRIMARY SOURCES

1. Books and Booklets by Liam O'Flaherty

*Thy Neighbour's Wife.* London: Jonathan Cape, 1923; New York: Boni and Liveright, 1924.

*The Black Soul.* London: Jonathan Cape, 1924; New York: Boni and Liveright, 1925.

*Spring Sowing.* London: Jonathan Cape, 1924; New York: Knopf, 1926.

*The Informer.* London: Jonathan Cape, 1925; New York: Knopf, 1925.

*Civil War.* London: E. Archer, 1925.

*The Terrorist.* London: E. Archer, 1926.

*Darkness: A Tragedy in Three Acts.* London: E. Archer, 1926.

*The Tent.* London: Jonathan Cape, 1926.

*Mr. Gilhooley.* London: Jonathan Cape, 1926; New York: Harcourt, Brace, 1927.

*The Child of God.* London: E. Archer, 1926.

*The Life of Tim Healy.* London: Jonathan Cape, 1927; New York: Harcourt, Brace, 1927.

*The Fairy-Goose and Two Other Stories.* London: Faber and Gwyer, 1927; New York: Crosby Gaige, 1927.

*The Assassin.* London: Jonathan Cape, 1928; New York: Harcourt, Brace, 1928.

*Red Barbara and Other Stories: The Mountain Tavern, Prey, The Oar.* London: Faber and Gwyer, Dulau and Co., 1928; New York: Crosby Gaige, 1928.

*The Mountain Tavern and Other Stories.* London: Jonathan Cape, 1929; New York: Harcourt, Brace, 1929.

*A Tourist's Guide to Ireland.* London: Mandrake Press, 1929.

*The House of Gold.* London: Jonathan Cape, 1929; New York: Harcourt, Brace, 1929.

*The Return of the Brute.* London: Mandrake Press, 1929; New York: Harcourt, Brace 1930.

*Joseph Conrad: An Appreciation*. Blue Moon Booklets, No. 1. London:
   E. Lahr, 1930.
*Two Years*. London: Jonathan Cape, 1930; New York: Harcourt, Brace,
   1930.
*The Ecstasy of Angus*. London: Joiner and Steele, 1931.
*A Cure for Unemployment*. Blue Moon Booklets, No. 8. London: E.
   Lahr, 1931; New York: Julian Press, 1931. In addition to the regular
   issue, E. Lahr also published a special spoof edition in 1931.
*I Went to Russia*. London: Jonathan Cape, 1931; New York: Harcourt,
   Brace, 1931.
*The Puritan*. London: Jonathan Cape, 1931; New York: Harcourt,
   Brace, 1932.
*The Wild Swan and Other Stories*. London: Joiner and Steele (W.
   Jackson), 1932.
*Skerrett*. London: Gollancz, Ltd., 1932; New York: R. Long and
   Richard R. Smith, Inc., 1932.
*The Martyr*. London: Gollancz, Ltd., 1933; New York: Macmillan,
   1933.
*Shame the Devil*. London: Grayson and Grayson, 1934.
*Hollywood Cemetery*. London: Gollancz, Ltd., 1935.
*Famine*. London: Gollancz, Ltd., 1937; New York: Random House,
   1937.
*The Short Stories of Liam O'Flaherty*. London: Jonathan Cape, 1937.
*Land*. London: Gollancz, Ltd., 1946; New York: Random House,
   1946.
*Two Lovely Beasts and Other Stories*. London: Gollancz, Ltd., 1948;
   New York: Devin-Adair, 1950.
*Insurrection*. London: Gollancz, Ltd., 1950; Boston: Little, Brown,
   1951.
*Dúil*. [Desire]. Baile Átha Cliath [Dublin] : Sáirseal and Dill, 1953.
*The Stories of Liam O'Flaherty*. New York: Devin-Adair, 1956.


2. Essays and Letters by Liam O'Flaherty

"My Experiences (1896–1923)," *Now and Then*, No. 10 (December,
   1923), pp. 14–15.
"Thy Neighbour's Wife" [explanation of why this novel was written].
   From the dust jacket of the first British edition of *Thy Neighbour's
   Wife*. London: Cape, 1923. This commentary aroused controversy;
   cf. "The Blurb Again," *Now and Then*. No. 10 (December, 1923), p.
   11.
"Sinclair Lewis's *Free Air*," *The Irish Statesman*, II (April 5, 1924),
   116. [a book review]
"Adrien Le Corbeau's *The Forest Giant*," *The Irish Statesman*, II (April
   5, 1924), 116, 118. [a book review]

"Vera Brittain's *Not Without Honour.*" *The Irish Statesman*, II (April 5, 1924), 118. [a book review]

"H. G. Wells' *The Dream.*" *The Irish Statesman*, II (April 19, 1924), 178, 180. [a book review]

"Maupassant's *A Life.*" *The Irish Statesman*, II (June 7, 1924), 402, 404. [a book review]

"National Energy," *The Irish Statesman*, III (October 18, 1924), 171. [letter to editor]

"*Trimblerigg* by Laurence Housman," *Now and Then,* No. 14 (Christmas, 1924), pp. 29-30. [a book review]

"Mr. Tasker's Gods," *The Irish Statesman*, III (March 7, 1925), 827–28. [book review of a novel by T. F. Powys]

"A View of Irish Culture," *The Irish Statesman*, IV (June 20, 1925), 460–61. [letter to editor]

"The Plough and the Stars," *The Irish Statesman*, V (February 20, 1926), 739–40. [letter to editor]

"Fascism or Communism?" *The Irish Statesman*, VI (May 8, 1926), 231–32.

"Review of Ethel Mannin's *Sounding Brass.*" *The Irish Statesman*, VI (June 5, 1926), 360, 362.

"Literary Criticism in Ireland," *The Irish Statesman*, VI (September 4, 1926), 711. [letter to editor]

"Art Criticism," *The Irish Statesman*, IX (October 1, 1927), 83. [letter to editor]

"Writing in Gaelic," *The Irish Statesman*, IX (December 17, 1927), 348. [letter to editor]

"My Life of Adventure," *TP's Weekly*, X (October 20, 1928), 756.

"Joseph Conrad: An Appreciation," *A Conrad Memorial Library: The Collection of George T. Keating.* (New York, 1929). O'Flaherty's essay later published as a separate booklet (1930).

"Foreword," *The Stars, The World, and The Women.* by Rhys Davies (London, 1930), pp. 7–9.

"Introduction," *Six Cartoons by Alfred Lowe.* Sketches of James Matthew Barrie, Arnold Bennett, G. K. Chesterton, Rudyard Kipling, George Bernard Shaw, and H. G. Wells (London, 1930), pp. 7–8.

"Red Ship," *New Republic.* LXVIII (September 23, 1931), 147–50.

"Kingdom of Kerry," *Fortnightly Review*, CXXXVIII (August, 1932), 212–18.

"The Irish Censorship." *The American Spectator*, I (November, 1932), 2. This article is also available in *The American Spectator Yearbook*, ed. G. Jean Nathan, Theodore Dreiser, *et al.* (New York, 1934), pp. 131–34.

"Autobiographical Note," *Ten Contemporaries, Second Series*, ed. John

Gawsworth [pseud. of Terence Armstrong]. (London, 1933), pp. 139—43.
"Irish Housekeeping," *New Statesman and Nation*, XI (February 8, 1936), 186. [letter to editor]
"An Braon Broghach [The Dirty Drop]," *Comhar*, VIII (Baeltaine [May], 1949), 5, 30. [a book review]
"Briseann an Ducas [Nature Breaks]," *The Irish Press*, May 30, 1946, p. 2.
"Troideadar Go Foicmar [We Bravely Fought]." *The Irish Press*. June 6, 1946, p. 2.
Ag Casadh Le Pádraig Ó Conaire [Meeting Pádraig Ó Conaire]," *Comhar*, XII (Aibreán [April], 1953), 3—6.

3. Poems

"Samaointe i gcéin [Distant Thoughts]," *Dublin Magazine*, II (December, 1924), 330.
"Na Blátha Craige [Cliff Flowers]," *Nuabhéarsaiocht (1938—1949)*, ed. Sean O Tuama (Dublin, n.d.), p. 35.

4. Translation of a Short Story from the Gaelic

Pádraig Ó Conaire, "The Agony of the World," *The Adelphi*, III (September, 1925), 258—60.

5. Short Stories in Periodicals

"The Sniper," *The New Leader*, January 12, 1923, p. 10; *Scholastic*, LXIX (October 18, 1956), 18.
"The Cow's Death," *New Statesman*, XXI (June 30, 1923), 364; "Bás na Bó," *Fainne an lae*, (Iul [July] 18, 1925), p. 5.
"Blood Lust," *New Statesman*, XXI (August 4, 1923), 497—98.
"The Black Mare," *New Statesman*, XXII (November 3, 1923), 110—11.
"Two Dogs," *Spectator*, CXXXI (December 8, 1923), 893.
"The Salted Goat," *The Irish Statesman*, I (January 26, 1924), 616—17.
"The Bladder," *Nation* (London), XXXIV (March 22, 1924), 887.
"A Pig in the Bedroom," *The Irish Statesman*, II (March 29, 1924), 71—73.
"The Wild Sow," *New Statesman*, XXIII (April 26, 1924), 65—66.
"Going Into Exile," *Dublin Magazine*, I (April, 1924), 789—96. Also in *The Irish Press*, XVI (April 22, 1946, p. 10; April 23, 1946, p. 7).
"The Hook," *Dublin Magazine*, I (May, 1924), 871—73.
"Fód [Earth]," *Dublin Magazine*, I (May, 1924), 882—83.

"Wolf Lanigan's Death," *The Irish Statesman*, II (June 7, 1924), 391–93.

"The Landing," *Living Age*, CCCXXII (July 19, 1924), 136–39.

"A Pot of Gold," *The Irish Statesman*, II (July 26, 1924), 615–17.

"The Blackbird," *Nation* (London), XXXV (August 2, 1924), 563–64.

"A Red Petticoat," *To-Morrow*, I (August, 1924), 1, 3–4, 6.

"A Crow Fight," *Dublin Magazine*, II (September, 1924), 102–6.

"The Reaping Race," *Dublin Magazine*, II (November, 1924), 257–61.

"The Conger Eel," *Nation* (London), XXXVI (November 1, 1924), 183–84; also in *Dial*, LXXVIII (January, 1925), 5–7.

"The Foolish Butterfly," *The Adelphi*, II (November, 1924), 474–77; *Dial*, LXXVIII (May, 1925), 402–4.

"Fishing," *The Irish Statesman*, III (December 6, 1924), 392–94.

"The Flood," *Dublin Magazine*, II (January, 1925), 408–10; *Living Age*, CCCXXV (June 20, 1925), 642–43.

"The Outcast," *The Adelphi*, II (February, 1925), 725–30.

"An Fiach [The Hunt]," *Fainne an lae*, (Meitheamh [June] 27, 1925), p. 5.

"The Wild Goat's Kid," *Dublin Magazine*, II (July, 1925), 793–98; *Dial*, LXXIX (August, 1925), 137–43; *Golden Book Magazine*, V (April, 1927), 451–54.

"Daoine Bochta [Poor People]," *Fainne an lae*, (Lúnasa [August] 29, 1925), p. 5.

"An toanać [The Fair]," *Fainne an lae*,(Meán Fómhair [September] 5, 1925), p. 3.

"The Tent," *The Calendar of Modern Letters*, II (October, 1925), 104–111; *Irish Writing*, No. 16 (September, 1951), pp. 11–17. [The 1951 version of this story differs to a slight degree from the original version.]

"Civil War," *The New Coterie*, No. 1 (November, 1925), pp 60–66.

"The Wounded Cormorant," *Nation* (London), XXXVIII (November 28, 1925), 317–18.

"The Cake," *The Irish Statesman*, V (December 19, 1925), 455–57.

"Milking Time," *Dial*, LXXXIX (December, 1925), 491–94.

"The Lost Thrush," *The Chapbook (A Yearly Miscellany)*, ed. Harold Monro, No. 40 (1925), pp. 14–17.

"The Inquisition," *The Adelphi*, III (March, 1926), 666–73.

"Offerings," *Outlook* (London), LVII (March 13, 1926), 191.

"Your Honour," *Living Age*, CCCXXVIII (March 20, 1926), 643–45.

"The Terrorist," *The New Coterie*, No. 2 (Spring, 1926), pp. 52–56.

"Irish Pride," *Nash's Pall Mall Magazine*, XCVII (June, 1936), 39–45.

"The Child of God," *The New Coterie*, No. 5 (Spring, 1927), pp. 43–60.

"Mackerel for Sale," *London Mercury*, XV (February, 1927), 354–61.

"Prey," *Outlook* (London), LIX (June 4, 1927), 711—12; *Bookman* (New York), LXVI (October, 1927), 193—95.

"The Mountain Tavern," *The Monthly Criterion*, VI (August, 1927), 118—27.

"Tyrant," *Bookman* (New York), LXV (August, 1927), 691—94.

"An Ounce of Tobacco," *TP's Weekly*, VIII (October 8, 1927), 739—40.

"The Old Hunter," *Golden Book Magazine*, VI (October, 1927), 443—46; *Irish Writing*, No. 21 (November, 1952), pp. 17—23.

"The Oar," *Outlook* (London), LXI (January 14, 1928), 54—55.

"The Strange Disease," *The Bermondsey Book: A Quarterly Review of Life and Literature*, V (March—May, 1928), 32—37. Later included in *Seven Years' Harvest; an anthology of the Bermondsey Book, 1923—1930*, ed. Sidney Gutman (London, 1934).

"The Little White Dog," *Bookman* (New York), LXVII (April, 1928), 145—47.

"The Letter," *The Criterion*, VII (June, 1928), 58—63.

"Patsa or The Belly of Gold," *The London Aphrodite*, 1 (August, 1928), 29—34.

"Red Barbara," *The London Aphrodite*, 2 (October, 1928), 78—83.

"Secret Drinking," *This Quarter*, II (July—August—September, 1929), 109—14.

"Spring Sowing," *Golden Book Magazine*, XI (May, 1930), 36—38; *The Irish Press* (March 28, 1946), p. 7.

"Selling Pigs," *Golden Book Magazine*, XII (September, 1930), 54—56.

"Proclamation," *Yale Review*, NS XXI (September, 1931), 158—66.

"Lovers," *English Review*, LIII (September, 1931), 437—45; *Harper's*, CLXII (April, 1931), 528—32.

"Accident," *Fortnightly Review*, CXLIII (February, 1935), 155—67.

"Irish Ride," *Forum*, XCIV (December, 1935), 343—51; also appears in a shortened version with title "King of Inishcam," *Living Age*, CCCLVII (November, 1939), 236—43.

"His First Flight," *The Lilliput Annual*, I (July, 1937), 1—3; *Ireland of the Welcomes*, XVII (March—April, 1969), 32—39.

"The Stolen Ass," *Lilliput*, II (1938), 397—98, 400.

"The Strange Hen," *Lilliput*, II (1938), 146—48.

"The Mouse," *Lilliput*, III (1938), 248—50, 252—53; *Coronet*, V (January—February, 1939), 7—10.

"Galway Bay," *London Mercury*, XXXIX (January, 1939), 297—307.

"The Bath," *Story*, XVI (May—June, 1940), 9—19.

"Indian Summer," *Good Housekeeping*, CXX (May, 1945), 34—35.

"An Čula Nua [The New Suit]," *The Irish Press*, June 21, 1946, p. 2.

"The Lament," *Harper's Bazaar*, LXXV (April, 1941), 58—59, 114—17; *The Bell*, XII (July, 1946), 283—300.

"The Wedding," *The Bell*, XIII (October, 1946), 40—59.

"The Touch," *Irish Writing,* No. 1 (1946), pp. 50–58; *American Mercury,* LXIV (May, 1947), 549–56; *Comhar,* July, 1946.
"Two Lovely Beasts," *The Bell,* XIII (December, 1946), 4–30; *Story,* XXXI (November-December, 1947), 30–46.
"The Night Porter," *Story,* XXX (January–February, 1947), 23–32.
"Life," *American Mercury,* LXIV (February, 1947), 156–61.
"The Beggars," *The Bell,* XIII (March, 1947), 5–23.
"The Parting," *Irish Writing,* No. 6 (1948), pp. 35–43.
"The Pedlar's Revenge," *The Bell,* XVIII (June, 1952), 148–61; *Collier's,* CXXXII (July 25, 1953), 148–61.
"Enchanted Water," *Yale Review,* XLII (September, 1952), 46–53.
"Wild Man of County Galway," *Collier's,* CXXXI (April 18, 1953), 54–63.
"The Fanatic," *The Bell,* XVIII (Summer, 1953), 16–26; *Pick of Today's Short Stories 5,* ed. John Pudney (London, 1954).
"The Post Office," *The Bell,* XIX (April, 1954), 5–26.
"The Blow," *The Bell,* XIX (May, 1954), 9–22.
"Desire," *The Bell,* XIX (July, 1954), 48–50.

## SECONDARY SOURCES

1. Bibliography

DOYLE, PAUL A. "A Liam O'Flaherty Checklist," *Twentieth Century Literature,* XIII (April, 1967), 49–51. This standard bibliography of O'Flaherty's essays, poems, and short stories should be supplemented by the additional items enumerated in this book.

2. Doctoral Dissertations

CANEDO, ANTHONY. *Liam O'Flaherty: Introduction and Analysis.* University of Washington, 1965. Surveys O'Flaherty's entire career, focusing on his fiction. Stresses that O'Flaherty's novels are concerned primarily with alienation and emphasize the meaninglessness of life. Naturalism, determinism, and pessimism are found to be inherent in much of his writing.
ZNEIMER, JOHN. *Liam O'Flaherty: The Pattern of Spiritual Crisis in His Art.* University of Wisconsin, 1966. Views O'Flaherty's writings and discusses his literary theories in relation to the period in which he wrote. Basic O'Flaherty theme is conflict between nature and intellect. His characters struggle to find some meaning in a meaningless universe while death waits to seize mankind.

3. Critical Materials and Comments about Liam O'Flaherty

BATES, H.E. *The Modern Short Story*. Boston: The Writer, Inc., 1941. Praises O'Flaherty's short stories for their poetic energy and their ability to project with authority the primitiveness of the characters and the setting. Notes similarities between the works of O'Flaherty and de Maupassant.

CRAWFORD, JOHN. "Liam O'Flaherty's Black and White World," *The Irish Press*, August 1, 1953, p. 4. A review article which considers *Dúil*. Maintains that O'Flaherty writes Gaelic "fluently and gracefully" but insists that the same virtues and weaknesses present in his English works are also characteristic of his Gaelic stories. When O'Flaherty writes of primitive life, he uses a twofold approach; a simple view emphasizing the difficulty of peasant life and the scene observed by a sophisticated outsider. These two approaches clash and frequently cause the stories to have a disjointed effect.

DAVIES, RHYS. "Introduction." *The Wild Swan and Other Stories*. London: Joiner and Steele, Ltd., and Wm. Jackson, Ltd., 1932. Praises O'Flaherty for the poetic qualities of his writing, his sense of wonder and delight, and his ability to describe rural scenes and folk. Finds that on some occasions O'Flaherty's style is too bald and that he overemphasizes drama and story. Does not believe that O'Flaherty is at his best while describing city life.

DE BHALDRAITHE, TOMAS. "Ó Flaithearta–Aistritheoir," *Comhar*, XXVI (Bealtaine [May], 1967), 35–37. Of all the authors proficient in Gaelic, O'Flaherty has achieved the most success as an English writer. O'Flaherty's stories in Gaelic are confined to two periods: 1924–25 and 1946–52. It is difficult to ascertain if several of O'Flaherty's stories were first written in Gaelic or in English, but in several cases it can be theorized which language certain stories first appeared in by comparing the flavor and style of the Gaelic with the English version. De Bhaldraithe gives illustrations of this approach, with particular emphasis on the story "Teangabháil [The Touch]," which was most likely first written in Gaelic. De Bhaldraithe has adapted his article into English in order to make it more widely available; cf. "Liam O'Flaherty–Translator (?)," *Eire–Ireland*, III (Summer, 1968), 149–53.

FREYER, GRATTAN. "The Irish Contribution." *The Modern Age*. Ed. Boris Ford. Baltimore: Penguin, 1961. In a brief survey of O'Flaherty's work, Freyer praises *Famine, The Informer*, and *The Puritan* but stresses the "diffuse and uncontrolled" aspects found in the other novels. Finds O'Flaherty particularly effective when he writes about the Aran Islands.

GREENE, DAVID H. "New Heights," *Commonweal*, LXIV (June 29, 1956), 328. A review article about *The Stories of Liam O'Flaherty* which especially praises two new stories, "The Post Office" and

"The Mirror," for a dexterity of handling and a poetic intensity not found to the same degree in O'Flaherty's early writing.

GRIFFIN, GERALD. "Liam O'Flaherty." *The Wild Geese: Pen Portraits of Famous Irish Exiles*. London: Jarrolds, Ltd., 1938. Facts and impressions about O'Flaherty by a newspaperman acquaintance. This essay contains valuable data concerning O'Flaherty's participation in the Irish Civil War and some helpful comments about his personality.

HACKETT, FRANCIS. "Liam O'Flaherty As Novelist." *On Judging Books*. New York: John Day, 1947. Hackett reviews O'Flaherty's whole career briefly although he is chiefly concerned with discussing *Land*. Argues that O'Flaherty's philosophy has thwarted his development as a novelist. O'Flaherty's Naturalism and his concentration on violence and danger bring too much rant and melodrama into his work.

HATCHER, HARLAN. "Motion Picture Drama: Liam O'Flaherty." *Modern Drama*, Shorter Edition, New York: Harcourt, Brace, 1944. Hatcher discusses the rising importance of the cinema as an art form and the brilliance of the movie version of *The Informer*. Hatcher comments upon the pictorial nature of the scenario, the taut, concise dialogue, and the effective use of psychology. Following his prefatory essay, Hatcher prints the "Cutting Continuity" version of the script, pp. 199–265.

HUGHES, RILEY. "Two Irish Writers," *America*, LXXXIII (September 2, 1950), 560–61. Believes that O'Flaherty's greatest strength rests in the passion and energy he gives to both animate and inanimate creatures. The animal stories are perfect in their kind although limited in their artistic stature because of their subject matter.

HYNES, FRANK J. "The 'Troubles' in Ireland," *Saturday Review of Literature*, XXIX (May 25, 1946), 12. Believes that melodrama is O'Flaherty's forte. Especially praises O'Flaherty for narrative ability and his talent for grasping the drama present in difficult situations.

"Irish Revival Delights Liam O'Flaherty," *The Irish Press*, May 13, 1946, p. 4. An interview with O'Flaherty shortly after he returned to Ireland after being absent for six years. He praises the current interest in Gaelic, the writings of O Cadhain and Tomas Bairead in particular, and favors compulsory Gaelic. Wrote a number of short stories in Irish while in America. Wants Ireland to develop a film industry. Plans to go to Aran and stay there for some time.

JACOBS, LEWIS. *The Rise of the American Film: A Critical History*. New York: Harcourt, Brace, 1939. Jacobs stresses how every detail in *The Informer* intensifies each scene in the film and notes that an unusual "richness" results from the scenario's economy. "Mood, pace, character, and sound are blended into a fluid unity."

KELLEHER, JOHN V. "Irish Literature Today," *Atlantic Monthly* (March, 1945), 70–76. Contains a stimulating analysis of *Famine*. Kelleher maintains that this work unites the movement and brutality of the early novels with the element of sensitivity found in the short stories. He feels, however, that the escape-to-America motif at the end of the story weakens the universality of the work. This article was also printed in *The Bell*, X (July, 1945), 337–53.

KIELY, BENEDICT. "Liam O'Flaherty: A Story of Discontent," *The Month*, NS II (September, 1949), 183–93. Censures O'Flaherty for too much roaring and too much offering of remedies. Maintains that there is a morose and brooding side of O'Flaherty's genius which mars all of his novels except *Famine*.

————. *Modern Irish Fiction–A Critique*. Dublin: Golden Eagle Books, 1950. Stresses O'Flaherty's obsession with having his characters make wild romantic gestures. O'Flaherty is concerned with the earth and with the relationship of humans and animals to the earth. Human beings are frequently not in harmony with the earth, and, consequently, they suffer. Kiely considers O'Flaherty a Romantic who adopts a rough pose in order to protect his romanticism.

MACDONAGH, DONAGH. "Afterword." *The Informer*. New York: New American Library, 1961. Contains an excellent discussion of the background necessary to understand O'Flaherty's most publicized novel. Particularly perceptive in discussing the theme and implications of the informer stigma in Irish writing and history.

MERCIER, VIVIAN. "Introduction." *The Stories of Liam O'Flaherty*. New York: Devin-Adair, 1956. Notes O'Flaherty's affinities with John Millington Synge and D. H. Lawrence. Insists that O'Flaherty's principal subject is the relationship between man and nature; nature is ultimately the stronger although it can act both as man's friend and enemy.

————. "The Irish Short Story and Oral Tradition." *The Celtic Cross: Studies in Irish Culture and Literature*. Ed. R. B. Browne, William J. Roscelli, and Richard Loftus. Lafayette, Indiana: Purdue University Studies, 1964. This essay presents some valuable thoughts on the fact that O'Flaherty's work is so little influenced by Irish oral tradition. O'Flaherty writes for the eye rather than the ear, and since he is very literate in Gaelic, he has difficulty in writing acceptable English-language dialogue for his Aran Islanders.

————. "Man Against Nature: The Novels of Liam O'Flaherty," *Wascana Review*, I (No. 2, 1966), 37–46. O'Flaherty writes about man versus nature. Man should battle nature and not deny it. O'Flaherty's sympathies are with the natural man. O'Flaherty is ambivalent toward characters who attempt to improve the peasants' lot. Mercier is very critical of *The Informer*; he believes that only

*Famine, Skerrett,* and the short stories are effective. Theorizes that O'Flaherty has grown in mental stability in recent years and consequently has written less because the emotional demon that produced his work has declined. Yet some recent short stories suggest that O'Flaherty could have begun a new mellower creative career if he wished.

MURRAY, MICHAEL H. "Liam O'Flaherty and the Speaking Voice," *Studies in Short Fiction,* V (Winter, 1968), 154–62. Finds unevenness in O'Flaherty's short stories, yet he is still an excellent writer. When O'Flaherty fails he does so because he ceases to be a storyteller and becomes a propagandist for some viewpoint. He also fails when he unduly forces excessive and artificial symbolism upon his short stories.

NEOL [LEÓN Ó BROIN]. "An Dorchadas (*The Darkness*), an original play by Liam O'Flaherty." *Fainne an lae,* Márta [March] 13, 1926, p. 6. Praises the play for its freshness and its artistry and notes that the story flows in one terrifying crescendo from beginning to end. Lauds the effective use of Gaelic language in writing a tragic drama.

O'CONNOR, FRANK. "A Good Short Story Must Be News," *New York Times Book Review,* June 10, 1956, Sect. 7, pp. 1, 20. Compliments O'Flaherty for his "narrative impulse" and for his ability to portray the instinctual life of individuals. Finds O'Flaherty's Gaelic superior to his English and dislikes the monotony of O'Flaherty's story form.

——————. *The Lonely Voice: A Study of the Short Story.* Cleveland and New York: World Publishing Co., 1963. Claims that O'Flaherty is a fine short-story writer and an inferior novelist; that the more primitive O'Flaherty's characters are the more effectively he handles them; that O'Flaherty is a genius when he feels but a very weak writer when he thinks.

Ó CUAGÁIN, PROINSIAS. "Dúil san Ainmhí Téama I Scéalta Liam Ó Flaithearta [Desire in Animals: Themes in the Stories of Liam O'Flaherty], *Irisleabhar Mhá Nuad* (1968), pp. 49–55, 57–59. O'Flaherty's gift for the mystical gives a magical beauty and wonder to his study of nature and animal life. He is especially effective in handling the natural instinct which animals and people have in common. O'Flaherty is an important short-story writer because of the effectiveness of his style and his ability to write accurately of what he is portraying. O'Flaherty's novels are considered inferior to his shorter fiction.

O'FAOLAIN, SEAN. "Don Quixote O'Flaherty," *London Mercury,* XXXVII (December, 1937), 170–75. Asserts that O'Flaherty attacks such follies as prudery, hypocrisy, and political trickery and calls attention to the hatred which rages in his work. Stresses the fury and speed of his writing. Finds that O'Flaherty is neither a true

Realist, a true Romantic, nor a true Naturalist. Like Joyce, he is searching for an ideal Ireland, a Holy Grail vision of freedom and protection. This article also appears, with some additions and omissions, in *The Bell*, II (June, 1941), 28–36.

—————. "Fifty Years of Irish Writing," *Studies*, LI (Spring, 1962), 102–3. Maintains that with the exception of Joyce, O'Flaherty is about the only twentieth-century Irish writer who has produced some novels which must be considered superior.

ÓG, OSCAR. "The Gaelic Players," *The Irish Statesman*, V (March 6, 1926), 802. A commentary about O'Flaherty's play *Darkness*. The play is found to have two faults: (1) Too much takes place in a short amount of time. The drama needs development and elaboration, (2) Lack of dignity, particularly in the melodramatic third act. Nevertheless, "it is encouraging to find original Irish work of such promise being done."

PAUL-DUBOIS, L. "Un romancier realiste en Erin: M. Liam O'Flaherty," *Revue des Deux Mondes*, XXI (June 15, 1934), 884–904. A survey of the principal biographical events of O'Flaherty's life as well as a review of the highlight happenings and characters of his principal novels. O'Flaherty is especially talented in bringing out the internal torments of his characters; e.g., the frenzied jealousy of Gilhooley, the agony of the informer, the mental anguish of the assassin, and so on. Paul-Dubois notes the harsh ferociousness and violent realism in O'Flaherty's writing, but observes that there is also much imagination, idealism, and poetic sensibility present. In fact, Paul-Dubois believes that O'Flaherty uses violence and ferocity to mask the sensibility and compassion in his stories.

ROSATI, SALVATORE. "Letteratura Inglese," *Nuova Antologia*, Anno 69 (September 16, 1934), 317–19. A very favorable commentary upon some of O'Flaherty's books, most notably *The Black Soul* and *The House of Gold*, recently translated into Italian. Notes O'Flaherty's realism, his use of sensational plot occurrences, his emphasis on torrid passions and portraying people from the lowest strata of society, and his bitter vision of life. Lauds O'Flaherty's ability as a storyteller and his talent for creating atmosphere. Especially commends the marvelous "lyrical force" found in O'Flaherty's work.

SAUL, GEORGE BRANDON. "A Wild Sowing: The Short Stories of Liam O'Flaherty." *A Review of English Literature*, IV (July, 1963), 108–13. Stresses that O'Flaherty is at his best when he writes of peasants and animals who are close to the soil. Among O'Flaherty's defects are poor taste, theatricalism, tautology, and the use of clichés. Points out that O'Flaherty's writing has considerable impact and that his imagination is powerful and compelling. Believes that O'Flaherty's later stories have weakened in vitality.

STERNEMANN, JOSEPHINE. "Irische Geschichten: Novellen von Liam O'Flaherty," *Die Neue Rundschau*, XLII (April, 1931), 521—39. This article consists of three O'Flaherty short stories translated into German. The stories are "Civil War," "The Reaping Race," and "The Inquisition."

SWINNERTON, FRANK. "Liam O'Flaherty's New Novel," *Now and Then*, No. 34 (Winter, 1929), 28—29, An unusually enthusiastic commentary about *The House of Gold*, calling it the best book O'Flaherty has yet written. Although Swinnerton points out that the scene is limited and the theme savage and notes the presence of melodrama elements, he believes the melodramatic aspects are well controlled and praises the novel's poetic eloquence. The book is found to be exciting and suspenseful.

THEO. "Dorchadas-tuairim eile [*The Darkness*—another opinion]." *Fainne an lae*, Márta [March] 13, 1926, p. 6. Censures O'Flaherty's play primarily because the people of Western Ireland are not portrayed realistically. Their dismal thoughts and behavior are in the mind of the author rather than being naturally in the minds of the characters. O'Flaherty is accused of exaggerating and distorting, and, therefore, he does not present a valid picture of his subject matter.

TROY, WILLIAM. "Mr. O'Flaherty's Development," *Nation*, CXXXVII (August 9, 1933), 165. Argues that there has been a decline in O'Flaherty's work since about 1928 and attributes this deterioration to O'Flaherty's growing hatred of certain aspects of Irish life, especially his animosity toward the church. O'Flaherty's hatred distorts the truth of his presentation.

————. "The Position of Liam O'Flaherty," *The Bookman* [New York], LXIX (March, 1929), 7—11. Perceptive and appreciative discussion of O'Flaherty's early writing. Believes that O'Flaherty is neglected because of his stress on melodrama. Defends the use of melodrama when it is handled artistically and dictated by theme, temperament, and environment. Argues that the basic theme of O'Flaherty's work is the conflict between nature and the intellect. Analyzes several of O'Flaherty's works including *The Black Soul*, which Troy feels is the best of the early novels.

————. "Two Years," *The Bookman* [New York], LXXII (November, 1930), 322—23. A discussion of the first segment of O'Flaherty's autobiography, stressing O'Flaherty's protean and romantic nature. Finds O'Flaherty more effective in writing fiction since weaknesses of thought, inconsistencies of viewpoint, bravado, and self-deception cause a reader to question the author's sincerity.

WARREN, C. HENRY. "Liam O'Flaherty," *The Bookman* [London], LXXVII (January, 1930), 235—36. Declares that O'Flaherty's basic theme is the hounding of men; this hounding is done by poverty, laws, men, and life itself. Warren is particularly impressed by O'Flaherty's stories about animals.

# Index